GROWING & USING HERBS

in the Midwest

A regional guide for home gardeners
by Rosemary Divock, herbiere

Amherst Press
a division of Palmer Publications, Inc.
Amherst, Wisconsin

Amherst Press
A Division of Palmer Publications, Inc.
318 N Main
Amherst, Wisconsin 54406

Library of Congress Cataloging-in-Publication Data

Divock, Rosemary, 1941-
    Growing & using herbs in the Midwest: a regional guide
for home gardeners/by Rosemary Divock. — 1st ed.
        p.   cm.
    Includes bibliographical references (p. 236) and index.
    ISBN 0-942495-52-7
    1. Herb gardening—Middle West. 2. Herbs—Middle West.
3. Cookery (Herbs) 4. Herbs—Utilization. I. Title.
SB951.H5D57   1996
635' .7' 0977—dc20   96-19449
                                                          CIP

Printed in the United States of America.

Illustrated by Mary A. Sallmann
Photography by Bill Paulson

Herbal Bouquets of Thanks

*For my special friends who have been there when I needed
encouragement, inspiration and help with the day to day demands
in order to write this book.*

I give you a bouquet from the heart—

Angelica for inspiration
Bay laurel for victory
Lavender for devotion
Lemon verbena for love
Marjoram for joy
Mint for virtue
Parsley for festivity
Rosemary for remembrance
Sage for health
Thyme for courage

Tom
Nancy, Dot, Helen, Dawn, Marlene and Glenn

Table of Contents

Introduction

As we move toward the twenty-first century, gardening, and especially herb gardening, has become a favored activity of people with hobby farms, big backyards, windowsill planters, a few colorful pots or single strawberry jars. We have found that by planting our own food, we experience a sense of safety and security. We are able to make all the decisions regarding the cultivation and harvesting of the plants: whether chemical pesticides and fertilizers are used and whether preservatives are added. Herb gardening, specifically, enables us to eat healthier, using fresh or dried herbs to season our food rather than salt.

Gardening itself brings a sense of pleasure and enjoyment. It allows us to spend time at home by ourselves or with the whole family. And each time we prepare food using the plants we have grown, we share with others the bounty of our time and care.

Gardening also presents us with challenges. As all gardeners know, there are no two gardening seasons alike—thank goodness! There are always successes and then those that are a little less successful. This book was created to assist gardeners growing herbs in one of the most challenging areas of the country: the Midwest. Defined here as hardiness zones two through five in Minnesota, Wisconsin, Michigan, Iowa, Illinois, Indiana and Ohio, the Midwest provides even experienced gardeners with challenges. Snow, frost, wind, and pests all need to be contended with in the midwestern garden. But by knowing the plants, the best place to grow them, and methods of protection, anyone can grow a successful herb garden suited to their own space and resolution.

First, the choice must be made as to which herbs to plant. Herbs in Profile describes 25 herbs commonly grown in the Midwest. The monthly calendar takes the gardener through the twelve months of the herb-growing season: from the first arrival of the seed catalogs in January through the month of December and its many traditions. Planning what herbs to plant, considering their interrelationships with each other, building up a rich soil, starting seeds, dividing perennials, taking cuttings, harvesting, preserving and cooking will fill up an entire year.

The greatest delight in gardening is the fact that each year is another beginning. With the same anticipation as every gardener starts the new growing season, let's journey through a world filled with herbs, their scents, colors, flowers and tastes.

GROWING HERBS

Definitions

Annuals: These plants germinate, flower, set seed and die all within one growing season. Plant annuals outdoors after the last frost date in your area (see page 77 for zones).

Half-Hardy Annuals: These plants have the same life cycle as annuals but are more tender. Half-hardy annuals don't grow until the soil warms up; in the Midwest, plant outdoors in June.

Hardy Perennials: Perennials come up every year provided care, maintenance and cultural requirements are met. Hardy perennials can withstand midwestern winters if they are mulched and given some protection.

Tender Perennials: As perennials, these plants will come back each year, but they are more sensitive to cold midwestern winters. In the Midwest they must be planted in pots. The plants grow well outdoors from mid-May to early September but must be brought indoors for the winter months. They cannot withstand temperatures lower than 40 degrees.

Biennials: These plants are slow to germinate but will produce growth the first year. With protection, biennials will come back for a second year with smaller growth; they flower, go to seed and die. For continued supply, it's best to treat them as annuals and plant new seed every year.

HERBS IN PROFILE

Anise Hyssop (Licorice Mint)
Agastache foeniculum

This unusual plant has outstanding blooms and leaves that are sweetly anise scented and flavored. A handsome, hardy perennial, anise hyssop stands erect and usually reaches three to four feet in height. It is a star in a summer border garden. From June to September it is covered with two-inch-long spikes of tiny two-lipped flowers that might be a pinkish mauve or a dusky violet in color. When the plant is in full bloom, it looks like a giant candelabra topped with spiked flowers.

The leaves and bright lavender flowers smell and taste of anise, but the square stems and leaves that grow across from each other in pairs tell you it belongs to the *Lamiaceae* or mint family. The leaves look a bit like those of catnip, another mint family member, but are larger. Anise hyssop should have a place in the garden toward the back of a bed of herbs since it grows to a height of four feet. This plant is always surrounded by honeybees and butterflies when in flower.

Seeds can be started indoors in March and transplanted about mid-May, after the soil warms up and the temperature is above 50 degrees. It

Anise Hyssop

3

flourishes at temperatures between 50 and 85 degrees.

This plant prefers full sun but can stand some shade and likes well-drained, fertile soil. Anise hyssop grows easily from seed and the mature plants will provide plenty of volunteers to extend your plantings or to share with friends. It will die back in the October-November time frame. Then you merely cut the plant back to the soil line and let it take its winter's nap. In the spring, around March or April, new shoots will begin to once again reward you for the next season.

Anise hyssop can also be grown in pots where it can be brought indoors in September. Here it will die back in the same manner in which it does outdoors. Again, cut back to the soil line and water once a week. At first signs of new growth, in January or February, increase watering and fertilize monthly.

It can be harvested once the plants are at least eight inches in height. Harvest by cutting off the upper florets of leaves and flowers. This will also make the plant fill out and become bushy, as well as stimulate more production of flowers. (See page 122 for more harvesting details.)

A superior source of nectar, the anise hyssop will bring bees and butterflies from miles around. The flowers are delicious nibbled right off the plant and are attractive dessert garnishes. With their sweet flavor of anise and slight floral perfume, the flowers work well in baked goods, desserts, fresh fruit salads, sweet and sour marinades or in Chinese-style dishes.

If you've never had a cup of anise hyssop tea, make room in your garden for this plant. When collecting flowers for tea, the tiny anise hyssop corolla can be removed from its calyx for a delicate taste or the entire florets can be stripped from the stem for a larger yield and a stronger flavor. The full flavor of this herb can be captured in tea only by using either fresh or frozen leaves and flowers (see page 189 for tea preparation methods and page 124 for freezing methods). A delicate blend of mint and anise flavors, the tea is delicious hot or over ice and is great mixed with hibiscus flower tea or lemonade.

Anise hyssop is a plant that you should have in your garden for the flavor, color, and for the bees and butterflies.

Bay Laurel
Laurus nobilis

In the ancient world, bay laurel was a symbol of victory and honor. In Roman custom, heroes were adorned with crowns of bay leaves and letters announcing victory were wrapped in bay leaves. The bay tree is believed to be a healer and protector. It was believed that bay trees were never struck by lightning, and if planted near a house, they would protect it from evil. Today, bay laurel finds a home in herb gardens for its unique beauty and use in food preparation.

A tender perennial, the bay laurel tree is considered an evergreen; its leaves may be plucked in all seasons, including winter. Sometimes bay laurel is confused with the poisonous cherry laurel *(Pronos laurocerasus)*. It also has evergreen leaves, but the fruit is bright red and not dusky black like that of bay laurel.

The bay laurel leaves are dark green, narrow and smooth. They have a warm pungent aroma that is especially intense when the leaf is snapped and the essential oil is released. The flowers appear first as tiny hard buds which open to small creamy white blossoms. The purple berries that follow will turn black and hard when dried.

Bay Laurel

The bay tree is one of the outstanding features of the Mediterranean landscape, growing to a height of 60 feet or more. The limbs support a wealth of luxuriant foliage and greenish yellow flowers. In the Midwest, bay trees must be grown in tubs or large pots and brought indoors for winter. They can reach a height of eight feet when grown in pots. It is also possible to train them as central stems to create standards.

As with many herbs, bay prefers a light, loose soil with good drainage and full sun.

The tree remains green, but dormant, throughout winter. In early spring, new green leaves start emerging. After about eight weeks, cuttings can be taken from the hardened shoots (see page 63 for information on taking cuttings). Cuttings take about six weeks to form roots. This is one of the most difficult plants to propagate. If you choose to grown bay laurel from seed, plant them during early spring. For better success at growing bay laurel, buy a plant already established.

When caring for your plant, take note that bay leaves tend to get scales on their undersides. Scales are insects that look like small, brown, raised spots clustered on the underside of leaves. They feed by sucking the sap from the leaves, secreting a substance that attracts ants and promotes sooty mold. Twice a year, in the spring and fall, the leaves should be cleansed with a cotton ball dipped in either rubbing alcohol or scale-cide oil.

While the leaves can be picked year-round by cutting off individual leaves at the stem joint, August is the best month for drying. At this time of the year, the sun's energy is at its peak. This energy works with the chemicals in the leaves, through the process of photosynthesis, to make the leaves their most flavorful.

Used either dried or fresh, bay leaves have a pungency that enhances many foods. It is one of the four ingredients of bouquet garni. By itself, it flavors soups, stews and casseroles as well as boiled, baked and steamed poultry, fish and meat. Bay leaves are the only herbs whose flavor improves with longer cooking.

Borage
Borago officinalis

Borage is known as an herb to stimulate courage and to "exhilarate and make the mind glad." For these purposes, it was used in drinks and salads. The ancients considered it an important herb that would cheer the heart when taken as a tea.

Borage is an annual herb, but once planted it continues self-seeding for years to come. The plant grows on a stiff hollow stem to a height of two to three feet. The stems and large leaves are covered with white hair. The sprawling habit of the branches creates a rounded shape to the whole plant but makes it too unrefined in appearance to be planted in a formal garden. However, it suits an herb garden well, and it blends nicely with other plants in a wildflower garden. Its blue and pink star-shaped flowers have a black center and add some color and grace to the garden.

Borage seeds can be started indoors in early March, with transplants going into the ground in mid- to late May. Seeds can be planted directly into the soil; by keeping them well watered, germination will take place in three to four days.

Borage will do well in just about any garden soil, but for optimum growth, maintain a fairly rich medium. A manure compost is the best fertilizer. The soil should be loose and well aerated. Keep the soil moist, too. It is advantageous to interplant borage among your vegetables as it attracts bees for pollination. It is a very good companion in and among strawberries.

Borage grows well in pots indoors or outdoors. Provide it with a sunny spot, moisture, and a fertile potting medium and give the roots plenty of space in which to spread.

Young tender leaves and flowers should be harvested in the early part of the morning, before 11:00 A.M.,

Borage

and kept refrigerated until ready for use.

Borage has a cucumber flavor and while the leaves are prickly, they can be steamed or sauteed like spinach. You can also eat the stems peeled and chopped like celery. The leaves and stems enhance cheeses, fish, poultry, most vegetables, green salads, iced beverages, pickles and salad dressings. The flavor blends well with dill, mint and garlic. Borage can not be used dried or frozen. The best way to store it for a longer time is in flavored vinegar (see page 181 for information on making flavored vinegar).

Borage flowers can be used to decorate cakes and dips. It can be put into ice cubes for floating in a punch or to give a special presence to a glass of iced tea. Borage flowers are loved by bees and borage pollen results in an excellent honey.

Grow borage for courage. Grow borage for the flowers. Grow borage for the bees.

Chervil
Anthriscus cerefolium

Chervil has been known for years by European herbalists as an herb that cleanses the blood in the spring. It is believed that the body becomes deficient in nutrients during the winter months, and in the spring, herbalists prescribe eating greens for rejuvenation. In many parts of Europe, bowls of minced, fresh chervil leaves often accompany meals and are liberally sprinkled on salads, soups and stews.

There are two varieties of chervil—plain and curly. Both are hardy annuals that are a bit fussy about their place in the garden, but once established, they will do quite well and will self-sow readily. The plants can grow to two feet tall. The fragile foliage will lighten a shady corner of your garden all summer long. By day, chervil is not a gorgeous herb but looks like pale dainty parsley. At night, however, its silvery-white flowers glitter in the moonlight. There are times during its growing season that its lacy leaves turn a purple color and make for a colorful garnish on a plate.

Chervil seeds can be started indoors in February; in fact, it can be grown indoors in pots all winter long. The seeds can also be started outdoors; make furrows about one inch deep and sprinkle the seeds but do not cover with soil. They germinate quickly in a bed exposed to the sun and kept well watered. Use a misting spray to water or cover with cheesecloth, keeping the cloth damp and removing cloth once seeds germinate. Chervil grows best with some shade and likes a cooler temperature. Sowing seed every

Chervil

two weeks from April to July will give you an ample supply over the summer.

When chervil grows to three to four inches tall, begin to water and harvest continuously, keeping some of it at that height during the hottest summer months. The most difficult part of growing chervil is keeping the plants from bolting, or going to seed. When the plant bolts, it will stop growing. Continuous cuttings spur its growth and keep it from bolting. It will continue to grow outdoors until a frost.

Chervil's lively delicate flavor is a cross between parsley and licorice. It has found its way into many dishes, especially in France where chervil is held in high esteem along with parsley and tarragon. Its uses are endless—as seasoning to fish, oysters, poultry and eggs, and in salads and sauces, especially remoulades and ravigotes. It is also excellent with carrots, cucumbers, asparagus, avocados, mushrooms and potatoes. Many of chervil's essential oils evaporate in drying, so it is best used fresh or frozen.

It is an herb with a flavor and fragrance that are warm and cheering.

Chives
Allium schoenoprasum

Garlic Chives
A. tuberosum

Chives have been around for at least 3,000 years and are respected for their compatibility with virtually every kind of food. They are one of the most popular flavorings used in cooking. Whether you grow the basic round chives or the flat garlic chives, you will come to enjoy its flavor and fresh-cut aroma.

This hardy perennial grows in clumps and has grass-like tubular leaves about 12 inches tall that die down in late fall. Seeds can be started indoors in mid-February or outdoors in mid- to late April. Seeds started outdoors can be easily raised by cluster planting (planting about 20 or more seeds in one spot). You can also divide from an existing plant in early spring; use a shovel to dig up and divide the plant, then plant the new clump in another location. The slender, dark green leaves require minimal care and thrive on constant snipping. In the Midwest, they may need to be divided every three years because they spread. Dividing gives the plant the space it needs to grow and thrive. If you do not divide the plant, it will get crowded and parts of the plant will die off in its struggle to survive.

Chives can be grown as a low border; they add a great deal of color and texture when in bloom. Chives are a good companion to carrots, improving both the growth and flavor.

Chives

11

Pick out the flower heads of chives regularly, because if the plant becomes too profuse, it may die of exhaustion. Don't be reluctant to cut chives way back throughout the growing season. The more they are harvested, the better they will grow, especially during and after the second year. In late fall, extend the productivity of the crop by cutting them to the ground.

Chives can also grow well in containers, and it's one of the herbs that grows indoors in the winter months. Remember that it does take a rest in December.

The bright lavender blossoms of the common chive plant begin to appear in the garden in May. The flowers taste much like the leaves. The flavor seems a bit hot to the palate at first, but then a nice oniony taste lingers.

The pretty, white, feathery, sweetly-scented garlic chive blossoms appear about mid-August. The flavor of the garlic chive flower is a bit more pungent than that of the common chive. Garlic chives, also known as Chinese chives, have flat leaves with a mild garlic flavor.

Blossoms of both chives can be used in making herb vinegars or can be chopped and used in salads or as a garnish on a plate. A combination of sauteed asparagus, sesame seed and chopped chive blossoms makes a wonderful mid-spring vegetable combination.

All chives are high in vitamins A and C, and their flowers attract bees to the garden, so this popular and versatile herb is healthful for gardener and garden alike.

— ॐ —

Chive tea may be used as a spray for apple scab and for powdery mildew on gooseberries and cucumber.

Cilantro

Coriandrum sativum

Cilantro is the most widely used fresh herb in the world, turning up in foods of virtually every major cuisine. It is found in either the leaf form, cilantro, or the seed form, coriander (it is one of those strange herbs where the leaf and the seed are known by different names). Cilantro, also known as Chinese parsley, is one of the few herbs where the stem is chopped and eaten along with the leaves.

A word of caution: There are two different types of cilantro available. Mexican cilantro *(Eryngium foetidum)* has a strong odor and is sometimes called "stinkweed." You may want to use cilantro-coriander *(Coriandrum sativum)*, which has a less objectionable odor.

This half-hardy annual has bright green lower leaves that are aromatic and toothed; the upper leaves are feathery. Beginning in early summer, clusters of small pinkish-white flowers grow from the upper leaves. The plants reach a height of 12 to 18 inches.

Seeds can be started indoors in mid-February and outdoors, by cluster planting, in late April. Cilantro has a tendency to bolt, or go to seed, easily in the summer. Therefore, in order to have enough for cooking, plant a succession of plants each week. It grows well during the hot summer months in a light fertile soil in partial shade. It needs to be watered well to promote growth of its lower leaves. In the world of companion planting, cilantro has a reputation for repelling aphids while being immune to them itself. It helps anise to germinate but hinders the seed formation of fennel. In blossom, the herb is very attractive to bees.

Harvest the leaves and flowers whenever they are available, trimming off

Cilantro

the top growth to encourage the plant to produce new flavorsome leaves. If you primarily want the seeds, let the plant flower and, in late summer, cut off the seed heads when they are just turning brown.

The fresh, young, parsley-like leaves have a distinctive and unusual flavor. They are best used fresh and can be added to salads and vegetable dishes. Cilantro is an essential ingredient in Indian, Thai and, of course, Mexican cuisine.

Cilantro-coriander has four times more carotene than parsley, three times more calcium, more protein, minerals, riboflavin, vitamin B and niacin.

Dill
Anethum graveolens

Dill held a permanent spot in the ancient gardens of Athens and Rome. Fragrant dill garlands crowned war heroes on their return home, and aromatic wreaths of the yellow flowers hung in Roman banquet halls.

Dill is considered a tender annual, but it can certainly be treated as a perennial because it reseeds itself so easily. In fact, you'll find that not only the wind but also the birds will scatter the seed—and often to places where you don't want it.

There are several types of dill—common dill, dill bouquet and fern leaf dill. Common dill grows bigger and produces more seed heads. Dill bouquet and fern leaf dill produce a more compact, bushier plant that does not produce a profusion of seed heads like common dill. Any variety lends a graceful note to your herb garden. Its feathery bright green foliage grows three to four feet tall, and the stems are topped by delicate flat heads of tiny, greenish yellow flowers.

Dill grows best when the seed is sown directly into the soil; begin planting in late May and do so each week through midsummer for a continuous supply of leaves. It likes a well-drained soil and full sun. As a companion plant, dill grows well with cabbage, lettuce and onions. However, dill will stunt the growth of the carrots if planted nearby.

Fern Leaf Dill

The flavor of fresh dill leaves is a mixture of anise, parsley and celery with a distinctive green "bite." The aroma is a clean combination of mint, citrus and fennel with a touch of sea air. Dill seeds taste of caraway and anise.

Both the leaves and the seeds are popular culinary herbs. Most people are familiar with the use of the seed heads for pickling, but the fresh flavor of the fern leaves is wonderful too. They can be used with fish, cucumbers, herb butters, salads, green beans, cabbage, cauliflower and breads. Dill vinegar is particularly delicious when a little lemon and garlic are added to the bottle—and don't forget to include the seed head as well. Dill is best used fresh or frozen. To preserve its delicate flavor, snip it with scissors rather than rip it with a knife.

Medicinally, the seed is used in salt-free diets as it is rich in mineral salts. Dill is also good for digestion; it is said to be a stimulant for the appetite, it settles the stomach and has been used to relieve babies' colic. To strengthen your nails, crush dill and infuse in a bowl of water as a bath.

Go out to your garden, cut an armful of dill flower heads and put them into a vase of water for a dining table centerpiece. Cut the seed heads, dry them and use when making dried flower bouquets, baskets or herb wreaths. Be creative, be imaginative and enjoy the flavor and beauty of dill.

French Sorrel
Rumex scutatus

The Rumex genus is a divided family. The sorrels are the cultivated members; the docks are wild. Sorrel, a hardy perennial, is mentioned in many of the old herbals mainly as a pot or salad herb. There is no long list of ailments it was said to cure, although it did acquire a reputation for preventing scurvy as well as cooling inflammation and heat of the blood. The docks are used as medicinal plants. The root of yellow dock *(Rumex crispus)* was used by the American Indians on cuts and boils. Throughout history the roots have been used as a laxative and also as a remedy for anemia because they reputedly draw iron out of the soil. The leaves and the roots of both sorrel and dock are high in vitamin C.

French Sorrel

Spring and sorrel go hand in hand. French sorrel is the first green to grace the herb garden, and it is said to thaw out "frosted spirits." It has been a tradition in France to eat sorrel in the spring to quicken the blood and enliven the appetite.

There are differing types of sorrel. French sorrel, also known as Buckler leaf sorrel, has a small, shield-shaped, light green leaf and a gentle acidity. Broad leaf sorrel, also known as garden sorrel, has a longer, tongue-shaped leaf growing on tall stems that send up red-green flower spikes in the summer.

Sorrel can be propagated by planting seeds indoors in mid-February or by division of old plants in early spring. It grows in a fairly moist, rich soil in full sun. If plants are kept well-watered, they will need to be fertilized only when the leaf size gets smaller. The hot weather makes the leaves taste bitter so it's best to mulch around the plant to retain its moisture. Sorrel can be grown indoors in pots and will produce tasty leaves 11 months of the year.

In order to continue leaf production outdoors from late March through November, you must cut back the flower spikes all summer long. The leaves should be harvested frequently to keep them small for better flavor. Individual leaves or the entire plant can be cut to stimulate the growth of young leaves.

Both French sorrel and broad leaf sorrel can be used interchangeably. Their vitamin-rich leaves offer a sharp refreshing taste to welcome in spring; broad leaf sorrel is slightly more acidic in taste.

For salads, use the younger, smaller leaves, no larger than six inches, to spark your palate with its slightly sour flavor and lemony zest. The larger leaves are better cooked or combined with other foods. The French have devised a very elegant way to fashion a spring tonic—a cream sorrel soup. Not only can the leaves be used in soups and sauces, but they can be added to omelets, meats, fish and poultry or cooked like spinach. Sorrel leaves can be wrapped around a whole fish, such as salmon, or around a pork roast, then tightly wrapped in foil and baked. Sorrel is best used fresh, as it has particularly thin leaves that do not freeze or dry well.

French Tarragon
Artemisia dracunculus var. sativa

Tarragon is one of the royal herbs, in fact as well as in legend. The Romans named this herb dracunculus because its serpentine root structure suggested little dragons. Its multi-faceted flavor heralds rich associations—glowing tapestries and paintings of dragons, their scales gleaming as greenly as the plant in the garden. Through the centuries, it has become more used and respected for its regal presence in the kitchen. Today tarragon is most popular among the chefs of Europe, especially those in France.

Of the varieties of tarragon available, French tarragon, a hardy perennial, is the culinary herb of choice. It must be started from cuttings or root divisions as it does not set viable seed. The tarragon seeds that are sold are Russian tarragon, *A. dracunculoides*, a tasteless look-alike of no culinary merit. Mexican tarragon *(Tagetes lucida)* is sometimes substituted for French tarragon when the later is dormant or where winters are too warm for tarragon to thrive.

French Tarragon

Spring is the time to add tarragon to your garden. Buy rooted cuttings or small plants of French tarragon and set them about 18 inches apart, as this herb has a shallow lateral root system. It likes a well-drained rich soil, a bit on the sandy side, and a sunny spot free from the shadow of other plants. Fertilize twice a month, especially during the first few months after it has been transplanted. Tarragon plants will grow as tall as three feet.

In order to ensure the most flavorful tarragon, roots of established plants should be divided every two or three years. This should be done in the spring, before the new growth is three inches tall. Dig up the plant and carefully separate it into pieces, each with part of last year's stem and roots. Make plant divisions just as you would for new plants (see page 80). Any extras you may have will be greatly appreciated by gardening friends who like to cook.

Tarragon dies back to the ground each winter, even in mild climates. In cold midwestern climates it should be carefully protected with mulch. Mature plants can be potted and grown indoors, but they need artificial light, about 15 hours a day, to maintain vegetative growth.

Harvesting tarragon can begin after the plant has reached eight inches in height. Although only the leaves are used for cooking, cut the upper part of the stem to encourage bushing.

The rich, anise-like, peppery flavor of tarragon and its complex aroma of just-cut hay, mint and licorice enhance a great variety of foods. Classic in bearnaise, tartar and hollandaise sauces, its flavor complements avocado fillings, mayonnaise for fish dishes, salad dressings, light soups, tomatoes, omelets and scrambled eggs. It makes an excellent herb butter for vegetables, steaks, chops and grilled fish. Rub on chicken or mix with chicken stuffing. A light sprinkling goes with many simply prepared vegetables, notably peas, spinach, cauliflower and potatoes. Tarragon tastes best on its own or with the classic fine herbs: parsley, chervil and chives. The strong aromatics of rosemary, sage and thyme do not harmonize with it.

Fresh tarragon is more subtle than the dried and should be used accordingly. Heat brings out its flavor, so cooked dishes usually need less.

The best way to preserve tarragon is in vinegar (see page 181 for information on preparing vinegars); the flavor is true and long-lasting (until the next season's growth), but the texture and color are not the same as the fresh. Freezing sprigs in airtight plastic bags also gives fairly good results. To dry tarragon, place sprigs on a mesh screen in a shady, but warm, place. Drying emphasizes the hay aroma and licorice taste at the expense of the volatile oils; the dried herb will not be as rich in flavor as the fresh leaves.

French tarragon, and only French tarragon—there is no substitute. Be sure it's among the herbs in your garden for a season of magical flavors.

Greek Oregano
Origanum onites

In Greece, oregano grows freely on the hills, and its aroma fills the air in summer. Oregano, "joy-of-the-mountain" in Greek, has been labeled everything from wild marjoram to winter marjoram to wild oregano. Oregano's history goes back 1,300 years longer than marjoram's, when it was mainly used for the medicinal purpose of relieving toothaches. During the fourteenth century, Spaniards and Italians began using oregano in cooking, especially in meat and vegetable stews with shellfish. After World War II, spice merchants began promoting and importing oregano in quantity, making it one of the most popular dried herbs in the United States.

There are many different types of oregano. The sprawling *Origanum vulgare*, also known as wild marjoram, has dark pink flower heads and is more for ornamental gardening; it has very little flavor and is not a good choice for cooking. Most generic oregano seed is tasteless or a mixture of varieties. Greek oregano, a hardy perennial, is preferred for culinary use. While it can be grown from seed, Greek oregano and, its close relative, culinary marjoram are usually grown from cuttings; take care to buy these plants from competent and reliable growers.

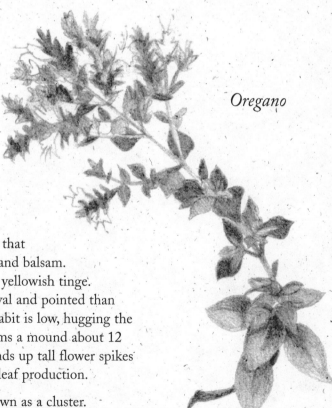

Oregano

The fragrance of Greek oregano is sharp and spicier than that of marjoram, with hints of clove and balsam. The fresh leaves are green with a yellowish tinge. The leaves are larger and more oval and pointed than those of marjoram. Its growing habit is low, hugging the soil. As summer progresses it forms a mound about 12 inches tall. In June and July it sends up tall flower spikes that should be cut for continued leaf production.

Greek oregano should be sown as a cluster. Germination is slow so keep the soil moist. Oregano likes a weed-free soil with good drainage and enough room around it for branching of its fine lateral roots. Fertilize once a month and pinch back new growth before it flowers for maximum leaf harvest.

Greek oregano grows well in pots for your winter indoor windowsill gardens. Start these plants in July and August to receive fresh herbs during the winter months.

Toward the end of the season, it's good to let some of your plants flower so that you can use them in herb vinegars and jellies as well as in herbal wreaths and dried bunches. Oregano dries well if the stems are cut and laid on screens or tied in bunches and hung upside down in a warm place. The sweetness of marjoram's aroma and the spiciness of oregano's complement one another equally well in the kitchen.

Lavender
Lavandula

Lavender has been the royal herb of Europe for centuries. Charles VI of France insisted on having cushions stuffed with lavender to sit on wherever he went. Queen Elizabeth I always had lavender on the royal table to use in sprinkling on meats and fruit dishes, as well as for teas.

I agree with Judy McLeod in her description of lavender, from her book *Lavender, Sweet Lavender:* "Close your eyes and sniff the scent of a lavender flower—drift into a dream of summer, a hazy glowing tapestry of flowers, a jungle thrumming with bees, alive with butterflies, sweet with sunshine..."

Lavender is classified as a perennial or tender perennial because not all types will winter in northern climates. Lavender "Munstead," which is a low-growing dwarf English lavender, is the most hardy for midwestern winters. It is excellent for edging paths, and it will produce many flowering spikes of either deep lavender-blue, white, pink or even green. Mature plants attain a height of two to two-and-one-half feet.

French and Italian lavenders, which are tender perennials, can be grown in pots outdoors then brought indoors to a sunny window for enjoyment during the winter months. They are one of the easiest plants to grow, but remember that even perennials take a rest in the dead of winter.

Lavender can be grown from seed or taken from cuttings of older plants in February or March. Seeds may take up to one month to germinate—be patient and keep the soil wet. When planting transplants outdoors in May, allow 24-inch spacing on each side for the plants to spread.

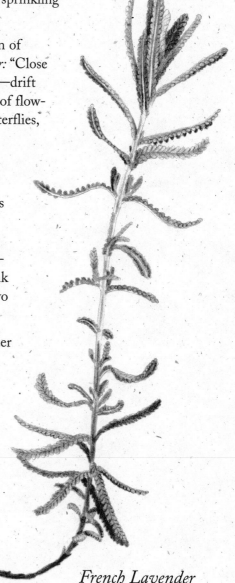

French Lavender

23

Excellent drainage and an alkaline soil will help lavender to grow well. They love the sun. Like all plants, they need a nutritional boost, and it is best supplied as a compost mulch applied regularly around the plant but not against the stem. In order to keep lavender plants from dying over the winter, put a small stone next to the root ball so that it will absorb the heat from the sun and keep the roots from freezing. Do not cut lavender back in the fall but leave it branchy. In the spring the new growth appears on the old wood. Pruning and trimming should be done at this time.

Lavender flowers should be harvested early to mid-morning to use fresh or to dry. If drying lavender, bunch together eight to ten spikes and hang upside down in a warm room with circulating air. You can then put them in a vase in a room, use in dried floral arrangements, or remove the flowers and make lavender water. Of all the flowers in existence, lavender retains its intoxicating fragrance the longest and has thus become the base for almost every potpourri recipe. Its aroma will bring the scent of summer to sachets too (see page 212 for making sachets).

The upper florets of leaves can be cut and used fresh or dried for cooking. It works well in sauces for salmon steaks or with fresh fruit and even in lavender cookies and ice cream (see page 204 for Lavender Ice Cream recipe).

There are so many things that you can do with lavender. Don't waste any time—go out to your garden and enjoy.

Lemon Grass
Cymbopogan citratus

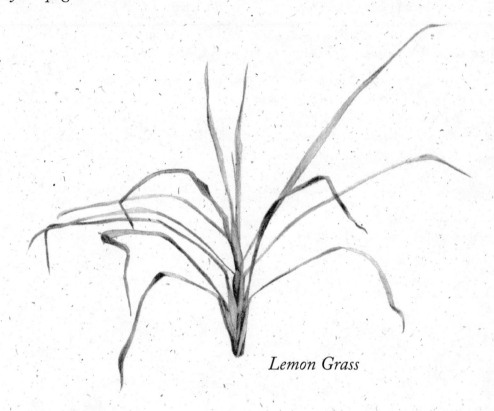

Lemon Grass

Lemon grass has long been grown commercially in Florida and California for its essential oils and as a base for citrus-flavored potpourris. With the increased interest in Oriental cooking, the tropical aromatic lemon grass has become a popular kitchen herb in our country. Its intense lemon taste enhances fish dishes and gives tea brewed with this herb a delightful flavor.

A native to Southeast Asia, lemon grass is a very tender perennial with its bulbs and dense bladed grasses growing above the soil line. In southern climates it reaches a height of three feet, like an ornamental grass, and can be left in the ground over the winter. In the Midwest it needs to be grown in a pot and transplanted to a larger pot as needed. Take lemon grass outdoors at the end of May and bring indoors in September for the winter months.

Lemon grass can only be grown from a root division, so you'll have to purchase a plant from a nursery or herb farm. Sometimes you may find it for sale, roots and all, in an ethnic produce market, in which case you can attempt propagation. Cut the blades down and plant the base in a moderately rich, moist soil. Within a few weeks, you should have a well-established clump of lemon grass. The bulbous clumps should be divided every second year to keep growth fresh and tender.

Harvesting may begin when the grass reaches 12 to 15 inches in height. Harvest at regular intervals thereafter, especially after the heavy growth begins in midsummer.

Its strong citrus tang has become a basic flavor for many Asian and Thai dishes. Because it remains fibrous even after lengthy cooking, it is best removed after it has imparted its flavor. If you have a surplus of lemon grass, you can chop it into half-inch pieces and dry it between paper towels. Add the dried herb to dried orange and lime rinds for a delicately scented, textured potpourri.

Lemon Verbena
Aloysia triphylla

There is little history or legend attached to lemon verbena, a tender perennial that was brought from Europe in the seventeenth century by the Spanish, who grew it for its perfume oil.

It is native to South America where it will grow outdoors to a height of up to 15 feet or more. In the Midwest it should be grown in pots and reaches a height of about two feet. Because it rarely forms seeds, propagate by taking three-inch cuttings of the new soft wood in late spring. It likes to grow in full sun in a slightly alkaline, light, well-drained soil.

Lemon verbena must be brought indoors in September for the winter; in November it will lose its leaves for its long winter's nap. At the sign of new leaf buds, around February or March, mist the plant with warm water and prune it modestly to encourage new growth. Take note that the new growth comes on the old wood, so you don't want to prune the thicker stems too drastically when you bring it in the fall.

Lemon Verbena

While indoors, lemon verbena is prone to whitefly and aphid infestations. To rid the plant of these pests, spray or wash all the leaves with insecticidal soap or liquid dish detergent late in the day. The next morning, rinse the leaves with water; a sprayer hose works well. When the plants are moved outside, at the end of May, the beneficial insects will keep the whiteflies and aphids to a minimum.

To keep the plant full and deep green, fertilize monthly from February to September and continuously prune branches, especially those that droop.

Leaves and clusters of leaves should be harvested from June through August as a part of its general pruning. It is at this time that lemon verbena leaves, the plant's most attractive feature, are at their most fragrant. The leaves release more oils during hot, humid weather. For the best flavor, harvest before the small, white clusters open.

Long, pointed and rough in texture, the leaves have a clean, sharp, lemony fragrance which is emitted with each contact. It is difficult to walk by and not touch or brush by the leaves to release that lemon smell. The flavor of the leaves is irresistible too. The fresh leaves can be used in marinades, beverages and salad dressings; the leaves are, however, too tough to eat and should be removed before serving. The leaves crumble easily when dried and the flavor takes readily to fish, poultry, muffins, sweet breads, jellies, jams, desserts and beverages.

Lovage
Levisticum officinale

In Europe during the Middle Ages, lovage was known as "love parsley" for its reputed aphrodisiac qualities. When the pilgrims came to America they brought the herb with them as a digestive aid. Today lovage is enjoying renewed popularity because of growing interest in vegetarian cooking. Its foliage has the properties of a yeast extract and can replace meat and bones in giving body to homemade soups.

Lovage, a hardy perennial, is a handsome plant that can grow to seven feet tall. Fresh ripe seeds can be sown in late summer and root cuttings can be taken in spring or autumn to propagate. Since lovage can grow to such a height, care must be taken to space the plants about two feet apart. Lovage grows in full sun as well as partial shade. It likes a rich, moist, well-drained soil.

The leaves, seeds and roots of lovage can all be harvested for use. Leaves can be picked all summer long as needed, picking the outer leaves first, trying to keep the center cluster of leaves flourishing for a continued supply. Gather seeds when they are ripe and dig the roots of your second- and third-season plants before the blooms open. To preserve, the leaves can be dried or frozen; the seeds and roots should be dried.

If you've never eaten lovage, use it cautiously at first. A little goes a long way. The unique flavor is a sweet combination of anise and celery that spans both traditional and mod-

Lovage

ern uses. Most commonly its celery-like stems and leaves are added to the stock of soups and stews where it adds a strong flavor to savory dishes. In addition, the leaves can be used in salads, stuffing and omelets. For people on restricted diets or for cooks interested in reducing their reliance on salt to flavor food, lovage alone or in combination with other flavorful herbs is an option. Lovage, savory, parsley, marjoram, thyme, basil and bay leaves make a good combination, fresh or dried, to flavor many dishes in place of salt.

The seeds, which are brown and crescent shaped, can be used to flavor liqueurs and cordials or crushed in breads or pastries. They can also be sprinkled on salads, rice or mashed potatoes.

Early herbalists recommended lovage, especially its roots, as a cure for many ailments including minor stomach complaints, kidney problems and headaches. In the seventeenth century the herbalist Culpepper recommended, "half a dram of the powdered root, taken in wine to warm a cold stomach, helps digestion, and consumes all raw moisture therein." The seeds, leaves and roots were steeped in water to make a tea taken as an aid to rheumatism. They can also be infused (steeped in water for a period of time, straining out the leaves and reserving the liquid) and used as a room deodorizer.

Lovage is an herb that is hard to find and is best to grow in your own garden. Once you've experienced the flavor, you'll find many more uses for it in your cooking.

Mints
Mentha

Mint's history goes back to medieval times when it was strewn on the floor of kitchens and sick rooms to sweeten the smell of the air. In Rome, peppermint wreaths were used as crowns, and in Greece, mint leaves were rubbed on the dinner table to cleanse and refresh it before serving food. In the eighteenth century it became an important medicinal herb for colic and digestive disorders.

Hardy perennials, the members of the mint family number more than 600, the most common being spearmint, peppermint, orange mint, applemint, pineapple mint, lemon mint, English mint, pennyroyal, black peppermint and catnip. Mints can grow to a height of 36 inches and can become invasive if not contained. In small gardens they can be confined to small tubs or pots that can be sunk into the ground. This will contain the roots and runners and prevent them from taking over the garden. In any garden, different varieties must be planted away from each other to retain their individuality.

True mint plants should be purchased or taken from mature plant cuttings or root divisions. There are some mints, like catnip and pennyroyal, that can be started from seed indoors in the spring. Transplants can be planted outdoors in May. They prefer a good moist soil and will
grow in full sun or partial shade.

Spearmint

Mints can be snipped freely for kitchen use throughout the growing season. In early fall, just before flowering or when the lower leaves turn yellow, cut the plants back to the ground.

Mint can be used fresh, frozen or dried for teas, sauces, jellies and vinegars. Pennyroyal is best known and used as insect repellent for fleas on cats and dogs.

Myrtle
Myrtus communis

Myrtle, which originated in western Asia, is believed by the Arabs to be one of the three things that Adam took with him when he was cast out of paradise. According to Roman mythology, Venus wore a garland of myrtle when she rose from the sea. And it is an herb with a long history of legends and strong ties to wedded bliss. Myrtle has been symbolic of love and the emblem of marriage for centuries. In the language of flowers, myrtle stands for love, peace, home, restfulness, and love in absence.

Myrtle, a tender perennial shrub, can reach a height of 10 feet when grown outdoors. Because it is tender, in the Midwest, myrtle must be grown in pots and brought indoors for winter. It can be trained into a topiary that makes an outstanding display with its sweetly scented white blossoms that appear from August to September. The berries appear after flowering. Its shiny leaves stay green all year long.

Propagation can only be achieved by stem cuttings taken in mid- to late summer (see page 63 for information on stem cutting). It thrives in full sun and needs some protection from the wind.

Myrtle

Stems and leaves can be harvested at any time, although it is better to cut the plants during their summer growth period.

Myrtle, as a symbol of love, is one of the most important wedding herbs. A sprig of myrtle tied with pretty ribbon can be attached to an engagement announcement, as it travels well through the mail. Along with orange blossom and rosemary, myrtle has been used for centuries to decorate wedding halls, to fashion garlands and crowns and to enhance bridal bouquets.

Myrtle also has culinary, cosmetic, aromatic and medicinal uses. The flower buds can be sprinkled on fruit salads once the bitter green backing has been removed. Powdered buds can be used as a spice and the leaves can be stuffed inside roast pork after cooking. The berries, ground up, are reminiscent of the flavor of mild juniper berries.

Cosmetically, the flowers and leaves can be added to ointments for blemishes. With their sweet, spicy, orange fragrance, they can also be dried and used in potpourri mixtures. Ages ago the leaves were used as an astringent antiseptic when infused in water.

This plant is a wonderful addition to your garden, or grow it indoors where its spicy fragrance and glossy green leaves may be enjoyed daily.

Parsley
Petroselinum

Curly—*P. crispum*
Italian or Flat Leaf—*P. crispum var. neopolitanum*

The Romans, the first on record to eat parsley, served it at feasts to cleanse and refresh the palate. But a thousand years before, the Greeks made wreaths of it for weddings and athletic games and fed it to their horses before battle to ensure valor.

Parsley is a biennial. Second-year plants seem to have more finely divided leaves and a grassier flavor. Mature plants will grow to about 12 inches tall.

Parsley will reseed itself, but to ensure an abundance, sow parsley every year, indoors in March and outdoors in May. The two most common types of parsley, curly and flat Italian, can be grown from seeds planted in clusters. Because they are slow to sprout, the seeds can be soaked overnight to foster germination. Sprouting varies anywhere from a week to 24 days. Parsley grows well in sun but some shade helps to develop a deeper green color. It is a heavy feeder, requiring plenty of water and fertilizer.

Both parsleys are quite hardy and may be harvested in winter even though the leaves are frozen. In the summer when other herbs are blooming or have gone to seed, parsley, a seasoned standby, is in the wings, ready for use at a moment's notice. It is also a good herb to grow indoors for year-round use.

Harvest parsley by cutting stems about one inch above ground level and taking the

Italian Parsley

outer ones first. The leaves as well as the stems of tender parsley may be used. Many cooks save the stems for stocks. Parsley is so easy to grow, and because so little of the real flavor of parsley is in the dried or frozen leaves, it is best used fresh. To keep your parsley fresh, store it in the refrigerator in a glass of water with the stems submerged and the leaves dry.

A bite of fresh parsley reveals its faint peppery tang and green apple aftertaste. The best tasting parsley is the flat leaf Italian type. It is gently piney and more aromatic than the curly type, although the curly keeps longer once picked. Whichever variety you use, the brilliant emerald leaves and mild yet piquant flavor makes it a counterpoint to most vegetables, fish, meats and soups. It is also one of the main herbs used in bouquet garni as well as in fine herb mixtures. It is an herb that is difficult to overuse.

Parsley is an herbal multi-vitamin. A cup of minced fresh parsley (about four ounces) contains more beta carotene than a large carrot, almost twice as much vitamin C as an orange, more calcium than a cup of milk and 20 times as much iron as one serving of liver. Parsley tea is a popular diuretic in Germany and China, where herbalists recommend it to help control high blood pressure.

If you are feeling tired and wilted, a parsley bath can help refresh you. Brew a strong parsley tea by steeping half a cup of bruised fresh parsley leaves in two cups of boiling water. Cover for 20 minutes then strain and stir into a drawn bath. For a quicker variation, pack a quarter cup of fresh parsley leaves into a large tea bale and hook it onto the bath faucet so that as the hot water comes out it runs through the parsley.

> *"The last to leave, yet rises early,*
> *it floats in pots and lies on plates,*
> *whether its shape is flat or curly,*
> *it's a character with pleasing traits."*
>
> —Susan Belsinger

ॐ

Over the years, parsley's slow germination has stimulated some fanciful theories. One of those is that it goes to the devil and back nine times before it sprouts. Another theory is that if a pregnant woman plants its seeds, it will speed germination.

Purslane
Portulaca oleracea

In the nineteenth century, purslane was a popular herb in French gardens and kitchens. The cookbooks of the time contained many recipes for its use; it was often cooked like spinach or prepared as au gratin. Today, while purslane is largely a neglected culinary herb, it is regaining its place in the kitchen due to its nutritional merits. Shepherd's Garden Seeds has cultivated a variety of purslane from France that is an exceptionally rich source of natural vitamin E and is high in Omega-3 fatty acids. These acids play an important role in reducing the risk of heart disease, arthritis and cancer. It has a more refined and delicate flavor than the common variety that grows weedily in gardens.

There are several types of purslane that can grow from seed. Summer purslane has been cultivated in India and the Middle East for years and was quite popular in Europe during the sixteenth century. It has either green or golden leaves that are small and spoon-like in shape and grow in a rosette shape from a fat juicy stem.

Summer purslane is considered a half-hardy annual, which means the seeds can be sown late in the spring, in May or June, and the plants will continue to produce into November. In order to get an early start, seeds can be sown indoors in early spring and transplanted outdoors after the danger of frost. It does well in light, well-drained soil in a sheltered south-facing position. It is best to cut it an inch or so above the soil, always leaving two leaves as the base for regrowth. The young growth must be picked continually or the leaves become tough. Both the leaves and stems are edible and combine well with hotter flavored leaves, such as lettuce mixes, nasturtiums and red mustard.

The second type of purslane that can grow from seed in the Midwest is called winter purslane, also known as claytonia or miner's lettuce. This hardy annual makes an indis-

Purslane

pensable plant for winter and early spring salad, providing several crops using the "cut and come again" principle.

For winter purslane, seeds need to broadcast in August or September. During the spring it grows very rapidly, producing narrow triangular leaves on short stems and pretty, edible, white flowers. It is always worth planting a few seedlings under cover in an unheated greenhouse in November, December or January. If the plants grow large enough, the first cuttings can be made in February, March or April. The plants remain small until early spring, then they will grow with extraordinary rapidity. As the plant gets older, its stalks become longer, its leaves more rounded and wrapped around the stem. The Germans, calling this plant winter portulaic, grow it as a seedling crop in greenhouses, harvesting the plants just before they grow their first true leaves.

Purslane is best raw or very lightly cooked and adds flavor to soups, scrambled eggs and Mexican tomato sauce. When used in cooking, add at the last minute to preserve its texture and flavor. Its slight hazelnut flavor also works well in many salads, mixed with leaf lettuces.

This is an herb worth cultivating for both its flavor and its contribution to your health.

Rosemary
Rosemarinus officinalis

Rosemary was once called the "Dew of the Sea" because it grew along the rocky cliffs of the Mediterranean. In ancient times, rosemary followed the bride throughout her life, from the cradle to the grave. It was planted in the bride's yard where it would thrive to give the newly wedded couple good luck and good life. Even today, the use of fresh rosemary for bridal bouquets and corsages is a traditional Croatian custom. It is said to be an emblem of fidelity.

One of rosemary's greatest virtues is its magical powers. It is known for its ability to restore the qualities of the mind of its wearers and users—to stir up the brain, improve the memory and add to the joy of life. There is a certain fragrance that it possesses that attracts all of us, an odor that is unmistakably rosemary.

There are numerous types of rosemary plants—ones that flower blue, pink or white and ones that grow upright or cascading. It is classified as a tender perennial and is not winter hardy for the midwestern climate so it must be brought indoors. Because it has to be brought in for the winter, it is best to keep in pots for ease in transporting. When grown in pots, a mature plant will reach a height of 24 inches.

Rosemary can be started from seed in early spring, taking up to a month to germinate. For larger starter plants, it is better to propagate new seedlings from cuttings of mature plants (see page 63 for information on taking cuttings). Rootings take ten days to three weeks to develop adequate root systems for transplanting. Rosemary likes to be planted in a loose, well-drained soil such as a soilless mix of peat moss, vermiculite and perlite.

The potted plants can be moved outdoors toward the end of May. The pots can be sunk in the ground

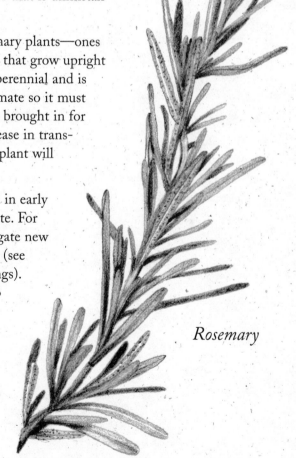

Rosemary

in a garden, then dug up in early September, washed off and brought indoors.

Rosemary flowers either in winter (January through March) or in the fall (August through October). After it flowers, all of the new growth starts and new cuttings can be made. It should be allowed to flower in order to stimulate new growth. For strong, vigorous plants, fertilize monthly, January through September, with a liquid fertilizer.

Harvest rosemary stems by cutting the newer growth—the white stems, not the woodier stems. Harvesting can be done at any time during the year.

Its aroma is gingery, spicy, sweet and faintly medicinal, all in one. It is the same, yet always different so that you are tempted to go back again and again to brush its leaves for the fragrance.

"Where rosemary flourishes, the woman rules," was a medieval saying from its use in kitchen gardens which were usually attended by women. Rosemary can be used in combination with many foods in the kitchen. For instance, a marinade for duck may consist of a blend of French tarragon, rosemary, Italian parsley, chopped onions and garlic, caraway seeds and olive oil. Rosemary can be placed under the skin of the duck when roasting, as well as in stuffing for poultry. Use it to flavor other meats and fish, too. It blends well with vegetables—baked carrots, peas, mashed or baked potatoes and squash—and with soups—lentil, mushroom, winter squash and vegetable soup. Rosemary drinks include wine, rosemary and cranberry cocktail and rosemary tea. It works well as a butter, in jelly and herbal vinegars, and best of all, in rosemary honey.

Rosemary can also be dried and used in potpourri blends for your bedroom or bathroom. Or better yet, add rosemary stems and needles to your bath water to increase blood circulation. It also works in easing the pain when applied directly to the skin since it increases the blood circulation and supply.

"Rosemary is for remembrance," and remember to use rosemary.

Sage
Salvia officinalis

There is an old medieval saying, "When all is well, sage will flourish. When things are going badly, it will hang its foliage." Back in the Middle Ages sage was considered to be a medicinal cure-all. It was even thought to impart wisdom and to improve the memory. It was valued for its properties of prolonging life, restoring energy and lifting the depression of the heart and mind. Sage is an Old English word which means "wise man."

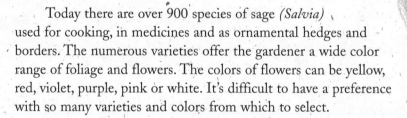

Sage

Today there are over 900 species of sage *(Salvia)* used for cooking, in medicines and as ornamental hedges and borders. The numerous varieties offer the gardener a wide color range of foliage and flowers. The colors of flowers can be yellow, red, violet, purple, pink or white. It's difficult to have a preference with so many varieties and colors from which to select.

Garden sage, the most common and frequently grown, is the cornerstone of the herb garden. It grows to a height of 30 inches and, in early summer, rewards us with beautiful violet flowers which are quite alluring to the bees. Garden sage is a hardy perennial, and it is one of the last survivors before taking a winter's rest. Sage can hold its own even after one or two hard frosts. In fact, some growers prefer to harvest sage after a hard freeze, believing that the flavor is superior then.

It can be grown from seed in early spring or from a cutting. Sage can be planted outdoors at the end of April, preferring full sun and thriving in well-drained soil. It is easily killed by overwatering and is drought tolerant once established. Sage planted next to cabbage will keep the cabbage butterfly away as well as make the cabbage plants more succulent and tasty. It is excellent to plant with carrots and rosemary. Don't plant sage near cucumbers—their chemistry does not mix.

41

In the fall, do not cut sage back, but wait until early spring to do some vigorous pruning that will encourage clouds of luscious purple flowers and full leafy growth. Sage plants will grow well for three to four years; after that, even under the best conditions, all the different types of sage will begin to decline.

Once plants are at least eight inches tall, they can be harvested from May right on up to Thanksgiving.

Fresh sage has a prominent lemon zest flavor. Because it was thought to be a digestive, it's easy to understand why it appears in dishes with pork, liver and sausage. It marries well with eggs and cheese and is outstanding with apples. Sage tea with honey added is good for colds and sore throats.

In Europe and the Mediterranean, where it grows wild with spiky lavender-blue flowers, sage is used extensively in cooking. In Italy, fresh sage leaves are fried whole and eaten with gnocchi (potatoes dumplings) and veal dishes. In England, fresh sage and onion stuffing is traditional with goose, and chopped fresh sage is mixed with cottage cheese to spread on dark bread. In Provence, sage is boiled with chestnuts and used to flavor watermelon preserves.

The zesty flavor of sage is lost when the herb is dried, but fresh sage can be preserved by placing sprigs in plastic zipper storage bags and freezing.

Bees are attracted to sage; sage honey is marvelous over homemade bread and muffins.

Pineapple sage *(Salvia rutilans)* is a tender perennial which must come indoors in September for the winter months. Here it flowers from mid-October until April.

The plants reach a mature size of four feet tall and three to four feet wide. Be sure to have a large enough area for your plant to grow indoors. Pineapple sage must be propagated from cuttings or root divisions; they can not be started from seed.

Although pineapple sage is a member of the sage *(Salvia)* family, its characteristics and coloring are quite different from common garden sage. Pineapple sage has fruit-scented, dark green, pointed leaves and blossoms that grow singly at the ends of the stems.

The brilliant red, long-throated flowers of pineapple sage have an aroma and taste similar to the common sage, but the floral aroma is stronger and the sage flavor is milder. The flowers can be cut with several leaves attached to use as garnish for fish, fruit salads or desserts. Pineapple sage leaves and flowers can be used with fish and chicken and in cheese, jams, jellies, teas, tea breads and a variety of desserts as well as in drinks.

Savory
Satureia

Summer Savory—*S. hortensis*
Winter Savory—*S. montana*

Summer savory and winter savory are related but have differing growing patterns, habits and flavors.

Summer savory is an annual plant which, when started from seed indoors, can be transplanted outdoors in late May and grows to 18 inches in height. Seed can also be directly sown when soil is warm. The mature plant has long, soft, bronzy green leaves, bushy stems and, in the late summer, small lilac flowers.

Winter savory is a perennial that is similar to summer savory in appearance and grows as a compact bush. It reaches a height of about 12 inches and has stiff stems that can make a low hedge for herb gardens. The glossy leaves are thin and narrow and its tiny white flowers appear in September through October. Winter savory can be propagated from seed but is slow to germinate, so multiplying by cuttings or plant division is preferred. Both summer and winter savory are good growing companions to beans and onions in the garden.

Fragrant herbs such as savory change priorities when they near flowering. They develop higher concentrations of essential oils, the flavoring and fragrance that has made them a part of the garden for centuries. Summer savory will slow or even stop growing after flowering. At the end of the season, allow it to flower, then cut and dry to use in herbal wreaths or bouquets. Its wonderful aroma will fill the house.

Winter savory should be harvested when the flower buds first form. It too can be allowed to go to full flowering, then cut and dried for herbal wreaths.

Both savories are cultivated for culinary as well as medicinal purposes. Summer and winter savory possess

Summer Savory

the sharp hot flavor that has earned it the name "pepper herb" and can easily replace pepper in the diet. In cooking, savories aid in the digestion of many foods, especially all varieties of beans. Savories are delicious with vegetables and will enhance stews, soups, gravies, sausage dishes, veal, pork and chicken stuffing. A sprig added to cabbage water will keep down the strong cabbage odor.

Remember that summer savory is sweeter than the spicy winter savory. Winter savory has the strong flavor of sage or thyme. Cooks use it more in the winter when preparing heavier dishes such as soups, stews and baked beans. The more delicate summer sister is used in the summer since it does not last when cool fall weather comes.

For many years, summer savory has been recognized as having medicinal value. A warm infusion tea is said to be a good remedy for a nervous headache if taken before going to bed. It is beneficial for colds and the oil is used to relieve toothaches. Crushed, it is good in an emergency to relieve the pain of bee stings. Winter savory possesses many of the same qualities.

Winter Savory

Scented geraniums
Pelargoniums

Rose, apple, lemon, lime, apricot, strawberry, coconut, peppermint—they sound like the flavors of candy sticks you might find in jars on the candy shop counter. But these are just a few fragrances in the amazing repertoire of scented geraniums. The unusual foliage, pretty blossoms and the delightful aromatic properties of these herbs have endeared them to gardeners the world over. And scented geraniums continue to grow in popularity as each year there are more new scents available.

Scented geraniums have been around for many centuries. The variety of scented geraniums is fascinating; differences in plant habit, leaf shape, texture, flower color and scent make for an astounding number of varieties to choose from. The shape of scented geraniums ranges from upright growers to cascading to slower growers. Leaf forms may be laced, divided like a pheasant's foot or a crow's foot, or shaped like a fan, an oak leaf, a maple leaf, a ruffle, a crisp ruff, a grape leaf, or a spreading umbrella. Their texture may be velvety or sticky. The flower colors include white, pale pink, lilac, orchid, scarlet, bright crimson and magenta. The scents include apple, apricot, coconut, lemon meringue, peach, prince of orange, strawberry lime, ginger, cinnamon, nutmeg, chocolate mint, peppermint, attar of roses, old-fashioned roses, lemon rose and citrosa.

Fair Ellen Scented Geranium

Classifying the vast number of scented geraniums can become a difficult task. Should they be grouped by habit of growth, leaf pattern or odor? The generalized groupings are usually by scent: rose, lemon, pungent, fruity, minty, spicy and large flowering. This last category is used because plants with large flowers usually have a weak scent.

All varieties of scented geraniums are tender perennials which must be brought indoors for the winter and are best kept in pots for this purpose. The plants stay green all winter long, giving off a pleasing odor as you brush by them.

Since scented geraniums do not produce seeds, the only way to propagate them is by cuttings from mature plants in early spring. Young potted plants can be moved outdoors at the end of May. They serve well as companion plants, keeping Japanese beetles away from roses, as well as repelling cabbage worms.

In early September, bring pots indoors and place in a sunny spot, like on a window sill, where your plants will give you many hours of visual and aromatic beauty. Once indoors, the plants will enter their resting stage. Plants should be cut halfway back in October to stimulate new growth in January. At this time, when you notice that they have come out of their dormant state and begin their new leaf growth, repot your plants, fertilize, and take some cuttings to be shared with fellow gardeners.

This new growth also spurs flowers—what a wonderful way to get through the months of January and February. The plants should be fertilized monthly from January through September to encourage new growth and flowers. The flowers of the scented geraniums are smaller and more delicate than those of the more common geraniums. The flowers and leaves can be cut from the plants all year long.

The uses of scented geraniums are many and varied. The oil from rose-scented geraniums can be used as an insecticide against red spiders and cotton aphids. Citrosa-scented geraniums are most popular for their mosquito repelling properties.

In addition both the leaves and flowers have culinary as well as medicinal uses. Why not try some scented geranium tea or jelly or scented sugar? It's fun to be able to pluck a few fresh leaves in the dead of winter for a special herbal treat—angel food cake with rose geranium jelly, geranium pudding cake or tea biscuits.

In the winter you can enjoy your own geranium bath oil, face cream or a rose-scented alcohol rub.

Sweet Basil
Ocimum basilicum

Basil, a tender annual, has become one of America's most popular fresh herbs and is therefore known as the king of herbs. Over the last few years, seed sources and specialty herb nurseries have introduced an assortment of basils to grow for various uses. There are now over 150 varieties to be used in pesto and salads or for drying, scents and ornamentation. The varieties include:

Sweet Basil

Sweet basil: the most familiar and widely grown. A strong bouquet best used fresh in sauces and for pesto.

Bush basils: shrub-like, a small leaf, good for pots or containers. Piccolo Fino Verde is preferred by chefs for its exceptional flavor.

Lettuce leaf basil: large, wide leaves, less pronounced flavor than sweet basil. Excellent for long-cooking sauces and for wrapping foods.

Purple basil: similar to sweet basil with a deep purple color. Grows slower and is wonderful for vinegars and pesto.

Scented basils: Cinnamon, licorice, anise, lemon, etc. for fruit salads, custards and sauces, as well as ornamentation.

Camphor basil: used in treating intestinal upsets and repelling mosquitoes.

Holy basil: has a pungent fragrance and is better suited for its aroma rather than to season a sauce.

Sweet basil, with its rich fragrant aroma and handsome, shiny, deep green leaves, is the basic basil for most culinary creations. The following techniques for growing sweet basil can be applied to all other basils with success.

Once established, the sweet basil plant will grow to a height of 18 to 24 inches. The seeds can be started indoors around the beginning of March, when there is more daylight and the sun it stronger.

Basil seedlings are extremely sensitive to wind damage, sun scald and cool temperatures. Before being left at the mercy of the elements, basil plants need to be hardened off (introduced to the outdoors gradually). To ensure continuous growth, don't set them out in the garden until night temperatures are reliably above 50 degrees and daytime temperatures above 70 degrees, about the end of May to early June.

Sweet basil may well be the original sun worshipper as it exhibits its best personality in the heat of midsummer. Make sure your basil patch is located where it will get at least six hours of full sun each day. Basil and tomatoes are good companion plants as basil helps tomatoes to overcome insects and disease. This marriage improves the growth and flavor of both.

Basil likes a soil that holds water and yet is well drained. Rain is the best moisture but Mother Nature does not parcel out that precious fluid in measured, regular amounts. Basil requires about one inch of water per week, and you must keep the roots mulched to retain moisture. Don't let the soil get so dry that the plant wilts.

Basil is crazy about the big "N"—nitrogen, which makes the leaves a deep rich green. During the growing season, it should be fertilized with a nitrogen mixture every two or three weeks for optimum production and flavor. Watch how your basil is responding to repeated cuttings in July and August. If re-growth slows down, respond with some growth power—fish emulsion or compost.

If you are eating basil regularly, you will automatically be doing a major part of basil maintenance—pruning. To keep basil plants well groomed and producing tasty, tender leaves at optimum levels, regular pruning is a must. Be sure to cut off all flower spikes before they get longer than an inch or two in length. Flavor changes begin to take place in the leaves when the flowering spikes are allowed to develop. Cut off the flowering spike just below the large leaf cluster, called the upper floret.

The best flavor comes from the oils, which are in top production when the climate is hot and humid. Harvest basil in June, July and August, once the plants are at least 6 inches tall (see page 122 for harvesting details). When September arrives, the temperatures cool down and basil growth slows. It is the first herb to bite the dust once the temperature drops to the low 40s, so harvest your basil early. Its tiny dark brown, almost black, seeds that are nestled in the withered basil flowers can be collected in September by shaking them into your hand. Thus, basil's unending life cycle will begin again next spring.

Basil can easily be grown in pots too, following the same harvesting and fertilizing procedures. Because it is grown in pots, it will need to be watered more frequently. Bring the plants indoors toward the end of August and be sure to place them where they will get sun all day. In the early fall as the days grow shorter, basil's growth slows down, and the plants get very leggy.

Growing winter basil is difficult because they prefer hot sunny days with lots of humidity, and these conditions cannot be created indoors.

Sweet Marjoram
Majorana hortensis

In mythology, marjoram is linked to love. The Romans began circulating the story that marjoram had been touched by Venus, who left its perfume to remind mortals of her beauty. It was used in love potions and bridal bouquets in France, Italy, Greece, Spain, Portugal and England. Italians gave nosegays of marjoram to banish sadness.

Sweet marjoram is an annual in the Midwest and must be started from seed, cuttings or transplants each year. February or March is the time to start new plants indoors by cluster sowing seeds. This means evenly sprinkling the seed across a four-inch pot then covering it with play sand (a fine sand) and misting daily until germination. About 10 to 20 seeds per pots will produce a nice size clump. Once the plants are three inches in height, you can begin to harden them off and plant them outdoors anytime after May 1. Mature marjoram will grow to be a foot tall.

The plants prefer full sun and well-drained soil and can be harvested once they are over six inches tall. In late summer, the plants will flower, bringing enjoyment to gardeners and bees alike.

Sweet Marjoram

Marjoram grows well in containers indoors during the winter too.

Sweet marjoram has a strong aroma that will hit you even before you cut it or stir it up. It has 30 or so cousins, with various growth patterns, but none with anything like sweet marjoram's distinctive flavor. Even the hardier wild marjoram simply doesn't have the coveted strong marjoram flavor.

Marjoram has long been a popular culinary herb. Its cultivation in the Mediterranean for over 12 centuries spread from North Africa and Southwest Asia. Recipes dating from the Renaissance call for marjoram in salads, in egg dishes, with rice, and with every variety of meat and fish. It was used to flavor beer before people started using hops and as a tea in England before Eastern teas were imported. Use marjoram grown indoors to flavor winter soups too.

The fragrance of marjoram is still prized by perfume and soap makers as well as by cooks.

Thyme
Thymus Vulgaris

In the language of flowers and herbs, *thymus* stands for courage. The Greeks enjoyed the fragrance of thyme and would bathe in it as well as use the oil of thyme for massages.

There are innumerable varieties of thyme, a low shrubby, hardy perennial. The plants range in height up to 12 inches, have a variety of different scents of leaves, and upright or creeping growth patterns. Among the varieties, the most commonly used are English thyme, also called winter thyme; French thyme, also called summer thyme; lemon thyme; and numerous creeping varieties.

All varieties of thyme have thin, woody stems and small oval-shaped leaves. In early summer they flower in colors that range from light pink to lilac and are favored by honey bees. Thyme likes to grow in full light in a well-drained soil. It can be grown from seed but is slow to germinate and slow to mature, so it is best to propagate from root divisions in the spring or stem cuttings at any time. Even though it is a hardy perennial, it may have to be replaced every two or three years as it has a tendency to become very woody.

Thyme works well planted anywhere in the garden, accenting the aromatic qualities of surrounding plants and herbs.

When harvesting the plants in late summer, be sure to leave several inches of woody stems above the ground, mulching plants for winter because the new growth sports from the old wood.

"When in doubt, use thyme." That is the herbal rule of thumb offered for confused cooks. Thyme tastes delicately green with a faint clove aftertaste. It

French Thyme

ranks as one of the fine herbs of French cuisine. It works well with veal, lamb, beef and poultry. Thyme also enhances stuffing, sausages, stews, soups, stocks, bread, batters and vinegars. Lemon thyme, an especially hardy variety, has a unique flavor that can be enjoyed in lemon bread, poultry stuffings or simply as a tea.

Thyme's medicinal reputation grew over centuries due to its antiseptic qualities. It has been used as a digestive drink to calm the stomach and for gastrointestinal complaints.

JANUARY

January To Do's

❦ Review last year's journal.

❦ Start a journal for this year; plan your companions.

❦ Review seed catalogs. See listing of herb catalogs in Resource Guide, page 234.

❦ Reorder seeds that have done well in the past and order new seeds based on your zone, light and soil.

❦ Begin to fertilize indoor herb plants at sign of new growth.

❦ Divide indoor perennials.

"Cold is the winter day, misty and dark;
The sunless sky with faded gleam is rent;
And patches of thick snow outlying mark,
The landscape with drear disfigurement."

—Robert Bridges

The name January comes from Janus, a two-faced god with one side looking backwards recalling the old, and the other looking forward to the new. Last season's failures have faded to dim memories, and hope springs eternal that the new gardening year will be successful.

This is the most optimistic month of the year on the gardener's calendar. It is filled with hours and hours of delight, plowing through all of the many seed and plant catalogs that come through the mail. It is that time of the year to think, plan and dream about your new spring garden.

Planning Your Herb Garden

The total planning process involves a sketch on paper of your garden that takes into account the interrelationships of the plants and a sense of height and color for a pleasing effect.

To get your creative juices flowing as you begin to plan your garden for the upcoming season, brew a cup hot herbal tea. There is nothing more reminiscent of your summer garden than the heady aroma of the herb leaves steeping in the water.

Rudyard Kipling described the scent of thyme on the Sussex downs as "like dawn in Paradise."

Gardening Journal

One of the best ways to begin your plans for the upcoming season is to keep a gardening journal. In this journal you'll want to record what seeds and plants you are going to use, where they were purchased, a diagram of your garden (especially how it was planted last year), brief notes about the climate throughout the season and finally, information on what was successful and what wasn't.

Last year's notes are essential for planning the new year's garden. Since there are many factors responsible for the success as well as the failure of your plants, a record of these successes and failures will help you to decipher what might work better in the future. If you've found success with specific seeds and plants, it's good to continue to use them; if you've had problems, it's good to determine why. Was it the climate? Was the soil too wet? Too dry?

When planning the diagram of the garden, there are important factors to consider. Many garden plans are based upon where the sun is coming from—the south. A plan should take into consideration placing short plants at the front (the south end) and tall ones at the back (the north end). By mixing flowers, vegetables and herbs, you can create a garden of fresh produce as well as a beautiful display. Take into account too that you will want to grow a variety of plants for an overall color spectrum during the entire season. (See page 102 for a sample kitchen garden.)

As you browse through the catalogs selecting seeds and plants, be sure to keep in mind the hardiness zone for your area. The hardiness map found in many of the catalogs dissects the United States and Canada into ten zones based upon the average minimum temperature for each zone. The Midwest falls into four zones—central states are in zone 5, and northern states are in zones 3 and 4, while the southern parts of the central states are in zone 6. While it is not as crucial for annuals, hardiness zones are very important to consider when ordering perennials.

Seed and plant companies located in the Midwest and other northern regions will have stock that is more winter hardy (see Resource Guide, page 234).

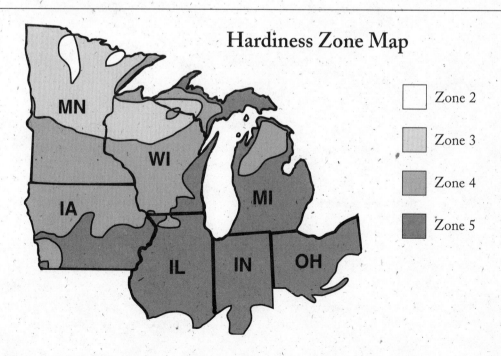

Hardiness Zone Map

Zone 2

Zone 3

Zone 4

Zone 5

Soil Structure

Establishing a good soil is one of the chief goals in gardening, so the next step in planning your garden is to examine your soil structure and determine the necessary amendments to establish a good soil. This may have to wait until March or April when the soil has thawed out.

In order to find out your soil structure, or the physical make-up of the soil and how easily water flows through it, take a handful of soil and squeeze it. If it crumbles very easily or runs through your fingers, it is sandy; if it holds together firmly, it is clay.

The ideal garden soil is loam, which is roughly half sand and half silt or clay, with a mixture of organic matter. There is a simple way to create loam without having to change the proportion of sand or clay in your soil—add organic matter.

There are many sources of organic matter—peat moss, leaf mold, rotted manure, leaves, grass clippings and compost. A cover crop of buckwheat or rye can be planted and tilled under to add more nutrients to the soil. (See page 134 for rebuilding the soil.)

Heavy clay soils hold nutrients and water well but they can become waterlogged, preventing plant roots from getting enough oxygen. Clay is hard to till and is a cold soil that warms up slowly in the spring. By adding the organic matter, you will create a lighter soil that drains well, warms up early in the spring and provides plenty of air, bacteria and other micro-organisms. The plant roots can penetrate this kind of mixture easily.

The Agricultural Extension Service offers to test your soil for composition of the basic nutrients as well as pH. The pH simply indicates the condition of the soil as to its acidity or alkalinity, expressed in units. It is important to know this because many plants thrive only when the pH value of the soil closely approximates the optimum for that particular plant.

A pH of 7 represents neutrality; higher readings indicate alkalinity, lower ones acidity. To neutralize acidity, the gardener can add agricultural lime. All soil, particularly alkaline ones, benefit from the use of compost or humus in the form of decomposed organic matter. Most herb plants survive well at 5.5 to 6.8 pH.

There is an old Chinese proverb that says, "He who plants a garden, plants happiness."

56

Companion Planting

The best gardening methods are creations of Mother Nature. It has been known for centuries that some plants grow better when certain other plants are growing nearby. Like the relationships between people, certain plants like and dislike each other, depending on the specific natures involved. The practice of growing complementary plants near each other is known as companion planting and is an important aspect to consider when planning your garden.

This is a part of the gardening world that has never been fully explored. It is the magic and mystery that has intrigued and fascinated people for centuries. Simply said, there are plants that assist each other to grow well; there are plants that repel insects; and there are even plants that repel other plants. Both root secretions and plant odor play a role in repelling and attracting.

These relationships become more important as adult plants develop distinct personalities, essences and aromas.

Companion planting and interplanting—mixing herbs, flowers and vegetables in the same area instead of planting the categories separately—are orderly ways to create natural diversity and encourage life and growth of all the plants. This controlled diversity permits you to maximize your gardening area's use of water, sun and, most importantly, soil nutrients. The placing together of plants having complementary physical demands over time is a kind of agricultural recycling. Known as "crop rotation," this method of planting returns as much nutritional matter to the soil as has been taken out.

The benefits achieved by planting basil and tomatoes together are a good example of the merits of companion and interplanting. A chemistry is released through the leaves as well as the roots that helps both plants grow strong and produce flavorful leaves and vegetables.

Herbs, for the most part, have a beneficial influence on the plant community. A great companion plant is dill. It is a good companion to cabbage, improving its health and growth. It does not do well by carrots and, if allowed to mature, will greatly reduce that crop.

———— ❧ ————

The Chinese called chives the "jewel among vegetables" for their marvelous health-giving properties.

57

Chives and carrots can be planted together for better flavor and growth. Apple scab, an age-old problem, can be prevented by planting chives among the apple trees. And when made into a tea, chives can be used as a spray for powdery mildew.

Thyme, which is a wonderful culinary herb, keeps away the cabbage worm. It can be planted anywhere in the garden, where it performs magic by bringing out the aromatic scents of plants and herbs.

Lemon balm is beneficial to the other plants around it and attracts bees. Both marjoram and oregano have a beneficial effect on surrounding plants.

Even plants that many gardeners consider to be a nuisance may be good companion plants. Stinging nettle, for example, has many benefits growing in the garden. It increases the essential oil content of most herbs, it stimulates humus formation and it helps stimulate fermentation in compost piles. As a fertilizer tea, it promotes plant growth and helps to strengthen plants. In fact, stinging nettles and tomatoes are good garden companions. The plant is rich in sulfur, calcium, potassium and iron. It's worth keeping them in your garden.

The dandelion increases the aromatic quality of all herbs, and in small amounts, it helps most vegetables. It has a high concentration of potash in its body and works to bring nutrients to the soil surface through its multifaceted root system.

Companion planting can also be used for insect control. You want the insects to know the plant is there, so use older plants with well-developed aroma and essential oil accumulations. The more "unpleasant" plants there are in the garden, the sooner harmful insects will get the idea that your garden is not a pleasant place to eat and propagate.

There are four different herbs that help to discourage the cabbage worm butterfly, although one herb may work better in your area than another. These herbs are hyssop, thyme, wormwood and southernwood.

Tansy should be planted under fruit trees because its scent deters flying insects and Japanese beetles. In the garden, it also keeps away striped cucumber beetles, squash bugs and ants.

❧

Savory is loved by bees and is ideal to grow near hives.

Horseradish should be planted at the corners of your potato patch to deter the potato bug.

Wormwood should be planted on its own since no plant grows well near it due to its toxic leaf and root excretions. However, used as a tea, it repels black fleas, discourages slugs, keeps beetles and weevils out of grain and combats aphids.

Probably the most beneficial and the real workhorse of companion plants is the marigold. When planted throughout the garden, it discourages Mexican bean beetles, nematodes and other insects.

By interplanting your garden, you will create an environment that will attract beneficial insects such as lady bug beetles, bright colored syrphid flies, lacewings, wasps and bees. The insects not only pollinate the fruits and flowers but also help to control aphids, mealy bugs and many other soft-bodied pests.

The use of a large number of herbs also fits in with the diversity of plant life favored by nature.

Companion planting is a fascinating field. It is one in which experimentation and research is continually being conducted to try to find answers to the many mysteries of nature. As in life, there are checks and balances in nature and we, as gardeners, continue to learn through our experiences. As you learn and read more about companion planting, the details will come naturally. Take it one step at a time. (See page 91 for additional information on companion planting.)

More of this gardening magic can be found in two paperback books: *Carrots Love Tomatoes* and *Roses Love Garlic* both by Louise Riotte.

Growing Herbs Indoors

A variety of herbs, such as chives, Greek oregano, rosemary, sage and thyme, can be grown 12 months a year. If you have a sun porch, sun room or solarium with a southern exposure, herbs can be grown throughout the winter months, keeping in mind that the perennials will all take a rest.

The plants you choose to grow indoors must be grown in pots from the start. By planting them in pots right away, the roots become acclimated to the pots and will continue to grow and thrive there. If planted in the ground, the roots will travel all over, and when dug up to be put in a pot, the plants go into shock. This will cause a setback in the growth of the plant, and it may not readjust.

Herb plants that are growing indoors will all show signs of life in the month of January. As the days get longer, lighter and sunnier, new growth begins to appear. At the first sign of this new growth, you can begin to fertilize the plants with sea mix, a blend of fish emulsion and seaweed that has a variety of nutrients and trace minerals important for the health and vigor of all plants.

Natural organic fertilizers promote growth at a natural pace. Some of the fertilizers available that promote fast, accelerated growth may produce larger plants but those plants will be less flavorful and have less essential oils. You want to use a fertilizer that gives natural growth and natural essential oil development. (See page 163 for details on container gardening.)

Dividing Plants

Now, when your potted perennials begin to awaken and show signs of new growth, is the ideal time to divide them. Division is not only the common method of propagating perennials, but as a gardener with a perennial border will confirm, most clumps remain vigorous and healthy only if they are divided frequently, every two or three years.

Whether you're dividing to grow in pots or dividing in the garden, the concept is the same. Dividing plants can be done by either root division or by tip cuttings from the new growth. Before you begin dividing, prepare the new homes for your divisions. The sooner you replant the divisions, the quicker they'll recover.

While indoor plants show their first growth in January, outdoor plants will awaken from their winter's nap in April or May. Division of these plants are taken then. (See page 63 for information on cuttings and page 80 for information on root divisions.)

FEBRUARY

February To Do's

❧ Start cuttings on tender perennials.

❧ Continue to fertilize indoor herb plants at sign of new growth.

❧ Gather supplies to start planting seeds—trays, pots, germination mix.

"Green fingers are the extensions of a verdant heart."

—Russell Page

The month of February is filled with excitement, love and romance.

For many centuries there has been a close association between the language of flowers and herbs and their meanings in romance, love and marriage. Ladies and gentlemen of the eighteenth century conducted affairs of the heart by sending tussie mussies. These are bouquets of colorful fresh or dried flowers, herbs and greenery. The bouquets are put together with a doily or stiff hanky as the base and given as a token of love, devotion and affection. Some of the flowers and herbs that were used to convey sentiments are:

Sweet marjoram: *"Your passion sends blushes to my cheeks."*

Lemon verbena: *"You have bewitched me."*

Feverfew: *"You light up my life."*

Angelica: *"Your love is my guiding star."*

Arborvitae: *"Live for me."*

Pansy: *"You occupy my thoughts."*

Sage: *"I will suffer all for you."*

Lemon thyme: *"My time with you is a pleasure."*

Coreopsis: *"It is love at first sight."*

Hollyhocks: *"You are my heart's ambition."*

Rosemary: *"Your presence revives me."*

Roses: *"I love you."*

ॐ

An old charm bids the bride and her groom to dip rosemary sprigs into their wine before they take their first sip, for then love will always flourish between them.

It is also in the month of February that some varieties of rosemary are blooming indoors, filling the plant with pretty pink, blue or white flowers. They must be allowed to bloom for this is the start of their new growth—first the flowers then the new stems. Other indoor and potted perennials will begin to show new growth now too. As was discussed in January, this new growth is the signal that the time is right for propagation. There are several forms of propagation you may use, one of which is taking cuttings from strong parent plants to start new plants.

Stem Cuttings

Herb plants that grow well when taken from a healthy parent plant are: bay laurel, curry, French tarragon, hyssop, lavender, lemon verbena, marjoram, myrtle, rosemary, rue, sage, santolinas, scented geraniums, thyme, winter savory and wormwood.

There are three types of stem cuttings that are suitable for herbs: softwood from new shoots which have not yet hardened; semi-hardwood from new growth when it has started to firm up at the base; and hardwood from woody shrubs and trees.

Softwood cuttings are taken in spring from strong new growth, or in late summer after flowering. Semi-hardwood cuttings are taken from plants such as myrtle in midsummer and mid-autumn. Hardwood cuttings are taken in mid- to late autumn.

The procedures are the same for all three types of cuttings.

1. The most important thing to remember is to keep your work area and tools sterilized. Use a sharp knife or pruning shears that have been dipped in a solution of nine parts water to one part bleach. Do not use scissors as they tend to pinch or seal off the end of the cutting, therefore making it harder for roots to grow from it.

2. Take cuttings from just below the leaf node, making a clean cut without ragged edges. For softwood cuttings, of plants such as French tarragon, scented geraniums and sage, cut a two- to four-inch piece of new growth with plenty of leaves. Trim off the lower third of leaves from the stem. Leaves left below the level of the mix will rot away, fostering a fungus condition that might spread to the stem itself. The semi-hardwood cutting should be from four to six inches in length and the hardwood cutting from six to 15 inches in length. When taking the hardwood cutting, cut off any soft growth from the tip of the cutting.

3. Trim off the cut edge, making sure it's a nice fresh cut, and dip just the cut tip in a powdered rooting medium such as Rootone. A rooting compound acts as a fungus

preventative—be sure not to get it on the stem as it
will prevent roots from forming up the stem.

4. Once you've taken your cuttings, prepare a mix of one
   part sand and one part vermiculite, packing it into clay
   or plastic pots with drainage holes. It's vital to use a
   highly drainable medium rather than a standard planting mix because cuttings, without any root system, are
   susceptible to root rot. Soil would keep the roots too
   wet too long.

5. Before you put your cuttings in, wet the mixture and
   pack it down so it's good and firm. Insert the stem
   about one inch into the soil mixture so it is standing
   erect. You can put numerous cuttings into a pot. Cover
   the pot with a plastic bag or cover and keep in a shaded spot.

6. Once you've inserted your cuttings in the pot, mist
   daily in early morning until the roots form. It is advis-
   able to remove the plastic cover every few days to
   change the air and prevent mold. You may also mist
   once a week with an organic fungicide, such as bor-
   deaux or copper fungicide, to prevent fungus and mold.

7. You can tell that roots have formed if you tug gently
   on the cutting and discover that it tugs back. Do not
   try this until two weeks after making the cutting.
   Constant premature tests will disturb the cutting.
   Rooting time can vary anywhere from two weeks for
   most herbs, to three weeks for rosemary and up to six
   weeks for bay laurel.

8. Once the roots are established, remove gently and
   transplant cuttings to pots containing your regular soil
   mixture, fertilize and move into a sunny location. Three
   to five weeks later, when plants are three to four inches
   high, pinch out the center of the young seedlings to
   make it bush out and become fuller and stronger.

❦

*In Victor Hugo's
words, "Life is a
flower of which
love is the honey."*

If you didn't bring in any plants, see if you can borrow cuttings from someone who has plants indoors; otherwise you'll simply have to wait until June to take cuttings from established plants in the garden. Another alternative would be to buy some strong, healthy plants in April or May from which you can make cuttings.

Scented Geraniums

In February the many varieties of scented geraniums are showing signs of new growth and flowering, too. These plants are tender perennials and differ from the ornamental geraniums in that they have more foliage (leaves) and smaller, daintier flowers. Scented geraniums are grouped with herbs because they are edible. Both the leaves and flowers can be used in cooking, in small quantities due to their intense fragrance. Foods such as lemon geranium cake, rose geranium ice cream, geranium butters and teas give a fresh and lively flavor to your meals. Interestingly enough, geraniums are rich in vitamin C. Face creams and bath oils can be made from scented geraniums, too.

At this time of the year, these plants are an exciting addition to your collection of indoor plants. Once you begin to explore the different types of geraniums you will be amazed at the choices available. Colors range from whites, yellows and creams tinged with yellow to pinks, reds, magentas and purple with some bicolor variations. The blossoms can be single or double. The leaves vary from tiny to huge, solid to deeply lobbed or lacy, shiny or dull or velvety. Some of the scents that are available include lemon, apple, orange, peppermint, pine and rose.

My favorites are the geraniums with strongly scented leaves; these not only smell wonderful but have beautiful blooms as well. Some of the highly scented geraniums have delicate flowers, while the softly scented varieties have larger flower clusters.

Scented geraniums need at least a half day of sunlight or artificial grow lights. They like a light, well-drained potting soil with some perlite added for aeration of the roots.

They should be fertilized twice a month. Water so that the soil is completely wet when excess runs out of pot, then allow to almost dry before next watering. Try to keep leaves dry and water at soil level. It's best to water earlier in the day. High humidity enhances their growth; to achieve this, place pots in waterproof trays of gravel filled with water, setting pots on top of gravel. This will also prevent the roots from rotting. Groom, trim and pinch some top growth to encourage bushing. Don't throw the leaves away—use some for jellies or potpourri.

Do take the time to touch the leaves and enjoy the aromas. After all, this is what makes them different from other plants, and what makes them great conversation pieces.

February is filled with color and scents that will get us through the winter blahs as we head toward spring.

Garden Notes:

MARCH

March To Do's

❧ Start your seeds and keep warm and moist. Be sure to put the date on plant markers and record in your journal.

❧ Move plants to light upon germination.

❧ Transplant seedlings to pots.

❧ Thin and fertilize plantings.

❧ Review garden plans on paper. Make changes, additions.

"The world's favorite season is in the spring."

—Edwin Way Teale

Spring is the transition between the extremes of winter and summer. Wherever there are four seasons, spring is synonymous with hope, youth and fresh beginnings. The world wakes then from the deep sleep of winter and new life rises from the ground. It is the season of procreation and renewal of vitality.

In the northern hemisphere the vernal equinox is March 21; it marks the official beginning of spring. In the southern hemisphere the spring equinox is usually September 22. On those days, the sun passes through the celestial equator—the line around the celestial sphere, the imaginary sphere projected into the heavens around the earth—and the world experiences a moment of equilibrium, with day and night everywhere on the planet equally balanced at 12 hours each.

Chervil was known for years by European herbalists as an herb that cleanses the blood in spring.

The equinox is the official start of spring, but the actual beginning—the day when new plant growth rises and migrating birds return—varies from place to place. The season moves north as the sun climbs higher, progressing, according to an old rule of thumb, at the rate of about 100 miles per week. For many people, especially those in northern regions where winters are long and rigorous, spring can not come fast enough.

The name itself has ancient roots and is mentioned in Old English texts as both the source of a stream and the act of leaping. In 1398, the word "springtime" was used to denote the season when the world leaps to its feet and new life springs from the ground.

One must have patience in the month of March. Certainly it is the most difficult month to get through because everything is just on the verge of coming to life. The maddening wait through the damp, cold weeks becomes frustrating.

Start Your Seeds

One antidote for the March gardening itch is to start your seeds. Seeds are a resting and survival stage in the continuance of a plant's existence. Starting seeds and following them through their stages of development is an exciting experience, one especially enjoyed by youngsters.

By strict botanical definition, a seed is a ripened, fertilized ovule containing an embryonic plant and a supply of stored food, all surrounded by a seed coat. Seeds are completely self-contained. Within the boundaries of their hard, dry, protective coat, they possess enough food energy to carry them through their dormancy and into their first few days as seedlings.

The time frame from when seeds are started to when the plant can move outdoors is important to consider. When moved outdoors, the plants should be in active growth and not overgrown or pot-bound. Remember that in the Midwest the Old Farmer's Almanac gives the last frost date as around May 20. This means sensitive plants can not be planted outdoors until after that date. Yes, some transplants can go out earlier than that date, but you must make sure to warm up the soil and have some protective covering over them. Otherwise they will go into shock and take longer than normal to mature.

Herbs such as chives, thyme and sage can be planted as early as mid-April, four weeks prior to the last frost date. Basil, chervil and cilantro need a warmer soil (at least 60 degrees) and should be planted several weeks after the last frost date, around June 1 or later. Study your seed catalogs, packets and gardening books to make sure you are planting outdoors at the right time. (See page 3, Herbs in Profile, for information on specific herbs.)

Planting Seeds Step by Step

1. Let's discuss the preparation of seeds before planting. The seeds arrive in paper or foil packets. A good rule is to immediately put them into your refrigerator until you are ready to start planting. By doing this, you will get the seeds ready to break their dormancy. That dormancy is broken when you take them from a cold environment and plant them in a warmer environment.

   When the dormancy is broken, the seed will begin to germinate. The longer a seed sits in wet soil before germinating, the greater the chances of mold, mildew and rotting. Before planting the seeds, you can take steps to help speed up the germination. For seeds with a hard coat, such as parsley, chives, borage and dill, striate the seed coat by nicking it with a knife or file. Don't cut too deep or you will damage the embryo.

Soaking the seeds for 12 to 24 hours prior to planting will also speed up germination. Pre-soaking seeds will cut several days off germination time for slow-to-sprout seeds like carrots, celery, parsley and chives. Some gardeners put seeds in small muslin bags and soak them overnight before planting.

2. Always sterilize pots and trays prior to starting new seeds. Mix one part laundry bleach to nine parts water in a large bucket. Dip trays and pots into this solution. This will help to rid your equipment of any fungus or eggs that can make gardening frustrating. Choose pots with drainage holes so that the seedlings will not get waterlogged. Shallow flats work well for seedlings that will soon be transplanted to larger containers.

3. Start with a loose planting medium. Seeds contain their own food supply so they don't need a rich soil right away. A good soilless or germination mix that consists of peat moss, vermiculite and perlite (some even have a fertilizer charge) is really the best way to start your new seeds. A soil high in organic matter used to start seeds may actually retard germination because of its higher concentration of carbon dioxide.

One of the best things about starting a variety of different plants from seed is that you're sure to succeed with something on your first try.

Put the soilless mix in a garden cart or wheelbarrow, and water it down thoroughly so that it's soaked before filling your pots and trays. Some of the mixes have a wetting agent mixed in, but if you fill the pots with this dry soil mix, watering only from the top will never get the soil soaking wet, which is what you want. Seeds germinate when they take on a quantity of water that swells the seed and makes it burst open.

4. Fill your containers with the loose medium and again water thoroughly before planting your seeds.

5. There are several ways to plant seeds. Scatter the seeds over the surface of a flat or plant them in rows. Either

way, be sure to give each seed at least ⅛ inch of space from its neighbor for small seeds, about ½ inch of room for medium seeds and about one inch of space for larger seeds.

Except for very fine seeds which may be pressed into the soil, seeds will need to be covered with soil. A rule of thumb is that seeds should be covered to a depth of three times their size. Some seeds do need light to germinate so it is important to read the seed packet.

6. The good thing about pre-soaking the growing medium is that now it's not necessary to water the planted seeds from the top. After planting the seeds, just cover the container using:

   – a damp newspaper or burlap

   – a scrap piece of aluminum foil

   – a plastic sheet or bag slipped around the flat (be sure to watch for mold on the soil—provide better ventilation if mold develops)

   – another seed flat

   – plastic cover made to fit on flat.

7. The most crucial time in the life of a seedling is this period just before it has broken dormancy. Each tentative little plant sprout is like a baby. It must have its needs met immediately. All of the factors that influence germination—water, air, temperature, light and soil conditions—must be kept in balance while we wait for the seeds to sprout.

Keep the seeds warm and moist. Most garden seeds will germinate at 65 to 78 degrees. Learn about your seeds and their temperature desires; keeping plants at even five to ten degrees below the ideal can mean many days in the emergence of seeds. Set the containers in a warm place where seeds can germinate—over a fluorescent light or near a furnace. In most cases, seeds need a warm soil to germinate, in a spot out of direct light. Because we soaked the soil earlier, there should not be a need to water prior to germination. If the soil is getting dry on the surface, use a mister to gently water. Check the soil daily for signs of mold; if mold does appear, uncover the tray for an hour or so to allow air to circulate.

Some seeds take longer to germinate than others; sage can take as long as six weeks to germinate while other plants' seeds make take only several days. But bottom heat and covers over the pots or trays, while keeping the seeds warm and moist, speeds germination.

8. As soon as the seeds germinate, move them to a bright, sunny window or greenhouse. They must be given light, either full sun, natural light or florescent grow lights. Temperature requirements are not as critical as light, but still important. Once the plants are growing above the ground, they need less warmth than is required for germination. In fact, seedlings grown in a cooler environment will make a better transition to colder outdoor temperatures. Plants grown indoors in warm rooms put on weak, spindly growth and will not make the transition well when brought outdoors, so keep them cool once they've germinated.

9. When your seedlings have their first true leaves, it's time to transplant them to pots of soil so that they can take advantage of the macronutrients and the microscopic soil life. The newly-emerged seedlings have absorbed enough of the seed's stored nutrients to get them off to a good start, but now your seedlings will need a richer growing medium.

Transplanting is more than a technique. It involves respect for the young life of the plant. The plant wants to grow; you might say it is programmed to grow. Having set the process in motion by planting the seeds, we now have the opportunity to give each seedling the most careful treatment so that it will continue growing smoothly on its way to producing our food.

Conditions often become crowded in the flats soon after the seed's leaves unfold. At this time, when plants are about one inch high, thinning must be done by cutting off every other plant or so. The extra plants should not be yanked out of the soil because there is considerable amount of root growth below the soil. The roots of the plants you want to save may be damaged by pulling out neighboring roots. There is more going on in the roots of even the youngest seedling than most of us realize. Roots not only anchor the plant and absorb nourishment, but they are also responsible for maintaining the pressure that enables the plant to raise water to its leaves and stems.

When choosing seedlings for transplanting, evaluating the root growth is as important as evaluating top growth. Look for a compact, well-developed root ball. A fringe of well-branched feeder roots will do far more for the developing plant than a single, thready trailing root.

10. After seedlings have been transplanted and develop their second set of true leaves, you should start to give them feedings every 10 days to two weeks. For these young seedlings, dilute the fertilizer by using three times more water than required for mature plants.

There are several types of fertilizers to feed your seedlings. Diluted organic fish emulsion contains trace minerals as well as the three major elements—nitrogen, phosphorus and potassium. Concentrated fish emulsion and seaweed can be purchased at your local garden center. Some gardeners use eggshell water (preferably not in the house unless you like the smell of rotten eggs) which is also a good source of nutrients for new seedlings.

Feedings of fertilizer can begin even earlier than when the second set of true leaves appear. These seedlings, growing in a soilless mix, should receive about two feedings of diluted fertilizer a week.

The trick now is to keep your plants growing steadily until it's time to prepare them for outdoor planting. We have begun the process of the rebirth of spring.

Garden Notes:

APRIL

April To Do's

❧ Have your soil tested and make a commitment to adding organic matter for a healthier soil.

❧ Propagate perennials by root division, cutting, or layering at the first signs of new growth.

❧ Begin to harden off hardy perennials prior to planting in the garden. Start warming your soil for planting.

❧ Use plant protecting tactics, such as location, mulch, cover crops and plant covers, to get your plants off to a strong start.

"A gardener's life
Is full of sweets and sours;
He gets the sunshine
When he needs the showers."

—Reginald Arkell

Spring Weather

We all have that urge to knead the soil with our hands and tools, to coax and nurse life from the earth. This urge comes from spending months scanning through the many seed catalogs. We are spring's impatient gardeners, anxious to get growing.

Yet in the Midwest, spring's impatient gardeners may likely find the fruits of their efforts wiped out in a single spell of bad weather. Beware the winds of March. They will dry out transplants, in addition to tearing tender stems and roots.

Then comes the April rains which drown the plants, cool and compact the ground, and can bruise the seedlings and wash out seedbeds.

And in a final holding action, May, June or even July frosts pass their cold judgment on gardening hopes. In one still night, seedlings, which represent weeks of nurturing, can die.

Gardeners have always been at the mercy of the elements which is why our forefathers were so acutely aware of the weather. But today, the gardener has several areas to draw upon when he wants to foresee upcoming weather forecasts. One source is the daily weather forecast with the extended forecast for the week. Another is the good old Farmer's Almanac, which gives the highs and lows as well as the last frost date by zones of the country. Each year this book gives the farmer all sorts of information related to the amount of rain, snow, and other weather conditions (based on the sunspot theory) by day, and by month, for 14 months. It is also a guide as to when to plant based upon the weather and the phases of the moon.

Another guide one can take into consideration is the "hardiness map" found in many seed and plant catalogs. This map neatly dissects the United States and Canada into 10 zones based upon the average annual minimum temperature for each zone. Even the greenhorn soon realizes that on a small scale map, it's impossible to show all of the minute climatic varieties within each zone.

Nevertheless, the 10 zones give gardeners a general idea of which plants will have a chance at survival in their area. The northern one-third of Minnesota and Wisconsin are in zone 3, where the average minimum temperature is -40 to -30 degrees. The southern two-thirds of Minnesota and Wisconsin, the northern third of Michigan and the upper half of Iowa are called the Northern Great Plains. Here winter temperatures start as early as October, and it doesn't really warm up until May—a shorter season. According to the hardiness map this area falls into zone 4, where the average minimum temperatures are from -30 degrees to -20 degrees.

The southern third of Wisconsin; the northern two-thirds of Illinois and Indiana; the southern two-thirds of Michigan; the northern half of Ohio; and the southern half of Iowa are in the Southern Great Lakes Region. Here winter sets in mid-November and begins to warm up at the end of March into April, for an average length growing season. According to the hardiness map this area falls into zone 5, where the average minimum temperatures are from -20 degrees to -10 degrees. (See Hardiness Map on page 55.)

Wyman's Gardening Encyclopedia states that "the hardiness of plants is based not only on a plant's resistance to minimum low temperatures, but to other factors as well, such as lack of water, exposure to wind and sun, soil conditions, length of growing season and with perennials, the amount of snow cover during the colder winter months."

With all these variables, it's no wonder gardeners cultivate an unhealthy skepticism of the broad-brushed zones. Micro-climates that include boggy areas or frost-prone valleys will have different conditions than other areas in the same general zone. Consult other gardeners in your neighborhood for specific climatic concerns.

Whatever the warnings about hardiness, growers seem determined to ignore them, developing an exaggerated estimation of their own expertise in the matter of local micro-climates. Even more dangerous is the gardener's recklessness in what is known as "pushing the hardiness zones." This irrational desire to cultivate plants that can not possibly survive local growing conditions has been called "horticultural bungee jumping."

The Soil

Growing strong, healthy plants is easy. All you must do is see that the plants get light, warmth, air, water and nutrients. The soil plays a major role in providing all of these things except for light. Soil is where it begins—where it has always begun. Tending to the soil is important everywhere we grow plants.

As the ground begins to thaw in April, this is an ideal time to have your soil tested. If you are starting a first-time herb garden, you will need to know your soil content.

Dig down about four inches in three or four spots in your garden, collect soil from each spot, and mix in a bag. This sample can be be tested at your local County Extension office. For a nominal fee they will send you a report as to the potassium, phosphorus and nitrogen content. This information, along with its pH level, will aid you in creating the best environment for your plants to grow (see page 56 for more details on soil content).

Excessive soil acidity is corrected by adding ground limestone or hydrated lime, worked into the top three or four inches of the soil uniformly. Excessive alkalinity is corrected by adding sulfur, aluminum sulfate or iron sulfate.

While these additives will neutralize your soil and allow a greater variety of plants to grow in it, the key to long-term management of the soil for nutrients and fertility is adding lots of organic matter. About 95 percent of soil consists of minerals, while only three to five percent of its total weight is organic matter. But never underestimate the importance of once-living material in the soil. It is something that must be renewed constantly if the soil is to stay in good condition. Organic matter is a major source of phosphorus and sulfur (major nutrients that plants require), the main source of energy for soil micro-organisms, and essentially the soil's only source of nitrogen.

The organic material will also benefit the soil drainage, its capacity to hold water, its microbial life and its aeration. No matter what type of rock particles predominate in the soil, the addition of organic matter will help improve its texture. In coarse sand, decaying matter will act as a sponge for water, reducing the tendency of the soil to dry quickly. A clay soil will be lightened

---

🪶

As Charles Dudley Warner wrote in 1829:

"To own a bit of ground, to scratch it with a hoe, or plant seeds and watch the renewal of life, this is the commonest delight of the race, the most satisfactory thing a man can do."

and made less soggy as organic matter helps open up and maintain a more porous structure.

Therefore, making and using humus, which is the decomposed organic matter in the soil, are the two most important things you can do to improve your garden. To build the humus in your soil, you'll want to add manure, rotted leaves, compost, and other organic matter to your soil at regular intervals (see pages 134, 136 for more on humus and compost).

Soil with organic matter not only provides nutrients for your plants but also provides a good home for organisms. "Living soil" is soil that has macro-organisms, such as earthworms, insects, mites and grubs, and micro-organisms, such as bacteria. These organisms work together to break down the organic matter in soil into nutrients the plants need to grow. One of the most beneficial life forms in the soil is the common earthworm, consuming large quantities of organic matter and soil particles, modifying them through digestion. "Dead soil" is that which has been sprayed with harmful chemicals to kill bugs. In addition to the bugs, the chemicals have killed many organisms that work to create healthy soil.

The use of organic amendments in the garden soil is an investment in the future. There is a golden rule among organic gardeners—a declaration that we put back into the soil everything we take out. Any gardener who practices this rule soon learns that he or she is not so much growing produce as growing soil. An organic garden is best understood as a soil garden. While it is a garden free of pesticides and chemical fertilizers, it is also a place where human beings begin to grow soil.

Organic gardening will bring us into the twenty-first century.

Propagating Perennials

We know that winter is over when, in mid-April, the already established plants from last year will be popping up with lush new growth. A walk in your garden in the next few weeks will bring to your attention new shoots forcing their way through the soil after being well-watered by the rains, reaching for the light. Start peeking under the salt hay, or whatever mulch you've used. It's not time to remove it yet, but where new growth is stirring, begin to lift the mulch little by little as the month progresses. Herbs such as chives, French sorrel, garlic chives, lavender, all of the mints, oregano, sage, tarragon and thyme are among the first to awaken from their long winter's nap.

Prepare these plants for spring by carefully clearing away dead debris, trying not to damage new shoots. Do not yet cut back sage, thyme, lavender or tarragon because the new growth starts on the old wood. Even though the plants might look like "death warmed over," new growth will suddenly appear. When you see the new growth sprouting from both the ground and from the old wood, you can selectively trim the dead wood branches.

Now is the time to divide your perennials. Dividing perennials should be done when it is best for the plant. In most cases, this is in early spring. The time will vary depending on the weather, anywhere from mid-April to mid-May. These perennials can be split when the plant starts to show signs of life in early spring, when the shoots are two to three inches tall. The exception to the early-spring rule is for those plants that bloom at this time. Plants that blossom prior to mid-May should be divided shortly after their blooming period so that the "operation" will not affect their blossoming the following year.

Root Division

Root division is the way to revitalize your favorite perennials for better blooms and to make more of them at the same time. Herbs such as chives, French sorrel, French tarragon, hyssop, mint, oregano, sage and thyme can be divided in the spring.

Before you begin dividing, prepare the new homes for the divisions by digging a hole and mixing compost into the soil. After making the divisions, quickly place the new plants in the hole, cover roots with soil, and water very thoroughly. The sooner the divisions are planted, the sooner they will adjust to their new home. If you're going to give the plants away, dampen some newspaper for wrapping the divisions.

When breaking apart a clump into manageable divisions, the best tools for the job are your own two hands. They are gentler and more sensitive than a spade or fork, especially when it comes to teasing apart tangled roots.

ॐ

After you've cleared the debris around your garden, it's time to come indoors and enjoy a cup of fresh herb tea made from the first shoots to appear.

There are two ways to take root divisions. If the original plant is too crowded for the space in which it is growing, it's best to lift the entire clump from the ground with a spade or garden fork. Loosen all sides before lifting and be sure to dig deep enough to get beneath the roots. If you're only dividing the plant, not relocating the entire thing, simply remove sections with a spade or fork while the mother plant remains in the ground relatively undisturbed.

Low-growing plants with small or shallow root systems, like creeping thyme and oregano, can be divided by hand. Simply break pieces from the clump or dig sections while the main plant remains in the ground. Always make sure two or three healthy growing shoots are attached to the division.

Plants with creeping roots, like mints, are even easier to divide. Just use a spade to remove a piece of the mother plant—stems, roots and soil—and plop it into the soil in a new spot. You can do this with or without digging the entire plant.

Deeper-rooted clumps, like sage, can be brought back to size by using a spade to slice off divisions from the outside of the plant.

Cuttings

Another method of dividing is by taking softwood stem cuttings of new spring growth. This method is more difficult in that the cuttings are not always easy to root. A good rule of thumb is to do these cuttings on cloudy, overcast days, preferably in the morning when it is cooler. Cuttings have a tendency to lose water through their leaves and quickly wilt, and if too many leaves are removed, the cuttings lose their source of food.

Softwood cuttings are taken with a sharp knife. Make a clean cut of a shoot with preferably at least three nodes—the points at which the leaves join the stem—so that the cutting will be three to four inches long. Do not remove the tip, but trim the bottom to just below the node. Take off the lowest pair of leaves or more so that a third to a half of the cutting is bare at the end.

To help induce rooting, use a hormone rooting powder such as Rootone or a liquid rooting compound. Place the mixture on the cut end but not up the stem. Cuttings should be planted quickly to avoid wilting. Insert them in pots or trays of wet soil-less mix or wet vermiculite or sand.

In order to root, the cuttings need high humidity and continuous warmth so it is best to keep covered with a plastic tray cover or plastic bag. Keep cuttings out of the sun, but not in heavy shade. When they have obviously rooted, showing signs of growth, the cover should be removed (see page 63 for more information on stem cuttings).

Layering

In addition to dividing your existing plants by root division and cuttings, you can also propagate them by layering. Layer woody stemmed herbs, such as upright thyme, lavender, sage, winter savory, rosemary, lemon verbena, and tarragon, in the spring for new plants in the summer.

Take a healthy outside stem and bend it toward the soil. "Wound" the part where the new roots will develop by gently rubbing some of the under bark off with a dull knife.

Anchor that section of the branch with a wire or a forked tree twig and cover the section with plenty of good soil and then a brick or heavy stone. Leave at least six inches of the end of the branch exposed to the air.

By late summer you should have several babies to cut from the mother plant to start lives of their own. Mulch them well for their first winter. Layering can also be done in late summer for transplanting in the spring.

Transplanting

If you are starting a new herb garden, it's best to start small plants in your garden instead of seed. Now is a good time to purchase the potted perennial herbs you would like to plant. "Harden off" these plants by gradually exposing them to the cool days of April. Leave them outside in a sunny location for longer periods each day for about a week before planting.

Parsley plants should never be given away, if you give away your parsley, you give away your luck.

If you moved potted hardy perennials indoors in the fall, you can begin to gradually hardened them off too. The tender perennials such as rosemary, bay laurel, pineapple sage and lemon verbena should not be moved outdoors until the danger of frost has past, mid-May to mid-June.

When the daytime temperatures are consistently in the mid-forties, you can begin to plant some hardy perennial herbs, watching them closely and giving them some protection when the weather takes a dip.

Be sure to let the soil warm up first before setting out transplants. This can be done by laying black plastic on the soil to heat it up for several weeks. Then poke holes in the plastic and plant the transplants. Pre-warming the soil will get your plants off to a good start.

Protecting Plants

As a gardener, you can not eliminate bad weather, but we can take steps that will greatly reduce the plant damage due to wind, rain and cold.

Location

Location is one of the most important factors affecting a plot's weather resistance, so the biggest decision you need to make is where to plant your garden.

Consider slopes. The crest of a hill is the windiest spot on it, and both water and cold air flow downhill and accumulate at the bottom. The hillside itself, then, is a better location than either the top or bottom.

Of course a southern slope is best. It gets more sun than most and is protected from cold northern winds. A westerly exposure heats up later in the morning than a direct southern one, thawing frozen plants more slowly and reducing possible damage. It also reaches higher overall temperatures than an eastern exposure, which makes an east or southeast spot better suited to heat-sensitive plants in summer.

Northern slopes receive the least amount of sunlight. Many people use this area to raise fruit trees. It's best to hold off planting on the northern slope as your spring plants will not grow well due to lack of sunlight and will certainly get wiped out by a late frost.

Buildings can create micro-climates of their own. The south side of a home offers shelter from northern winds. It also absorbs solar energy during the day and slowly releases that warmth at night. A permanent bed along the south wall would be a great place for your earliest starts.

Lakes and ponds reflect heat and light to plants grown nearby, but they also allow an unobstructed pathway for winds.

By building slopes or raised beds, bodies of water and surrounding vegetation, you can alter weather patterns dramatically; so much that you may have several different micro-climates on your property. It may actually be worthwhile to move an existing garden, if in so doing it would dramatically decrease the amount of energy you spend in confronting the elements.

Once you've picked the best site, consider building fences or rows of trees and shrubs arranged to give wind protection. Remember, wind inflicts direct punishment and increases cold damage and dehydration in dry weather. Reducing its effects is essential to early-season growing.

Mulch

A thick layer of mulch—straw, leaves, wood chips or other dead plant material laid on your garden—will definitely protect your plot from rain-caused erosion. But this insulation layer can also keep your soil from warming up quickly, so don't mulch heavily where you want to grow early spring crops.

A light mulch over a seedbed will cushion the scattering force of pounding raindrops, and a medium-depth mulch can prevent soil splatters on seedlings.

Cover Crop

Planting a cover crop in the fall sharply reduces wind and water damage. It improves the organic matter of your soil as well

---

ॐ

There is an old-time strategy that involves seeking out plants that originated in a climate type similar to the climate where you live. Plants genetically adapted to particular climate regimes will most readily adapt to similar growing conditions.

---

as helps to dry an early-season garden by drawing excess moisture out of the ground. Hardy crops such as hairy vetch, winter rye and fava beans planted in fall will help spring plots greatly (see page 143 for information on cover crops).

Individual Plant and Bed Protectors

Once you've done all you can to make your plot less vulnerable to nature's attacks, you can turn your attention to protecting individual plants or beds. These portable aids will help buffer wind, cold and rain well enough to make a significant difference in how well your crops survive bad weather.

Early in the 20th century, the French market gardeners used bell-shaped glass jars called cloches to protect their early crops. Nowadays most people use plastic milk jugs for the job. By cutting off the bottom you can put one over each plant you want to shelter. These miniature hot houses are free, durable and, equally important, easy to ventilate on sunny days—just unscrew the cap. If you live in a windy area, be sure to tie them to stakes.

You can also buy or construct cone-shaped plant protectors made of plastic or fiberglass. One such product, the Wall o' Water, has water-filled walls that absorb heat by day and release it at night. Old black tires can be used to shelter and warm seedlings, and if you grow your tomato plants in wire cages, you can wrap those supports with clear plastic during fickle weather weeks.

Many times it's easier to protect an entire garden bed by covering it with a material that breathes for ventilation. Proper ventilation is important because overheating and dampness induces plant diseases. A recent "space age" bed cover is Reemay, which is a spun-bond polyester or polypropylene. Light and rain easily penetrate this white porous fabric. Like plastic, this floating cover doesn't provide much direct frost protection, but the sheltered environment it creates can extend either end of the gardening season by a few weeks.

During the spring, short sharp frosts occur toward dawn. Plants can be protected from this type of frost by giving them a cold water shower from the garden sprinkler. The finer and more mist-like the spray, the better the effect. Plants can also be covered with old sheets and blankets that can be removed in the morning.

Springtime gardening will always be a gamble—who would really want it any other way? But you don't have to just set out your plants and take your chances. You can tilt the odds in your garden's favor. A creative grower will experiment with all of these garden protecting tactics, or better yet combine them.

Garden Notes:

MAY

May To Do's

୫ Celebrate May Day. Give away plants and cuttings to fellow gardeners.

୫ Make sure soil is turned and compost mixed in for active nutrients before planting.

୫ Start to harden off young transplants before planting outdoors.

୫ Review your garden plan to include companion planting.

୫ Check astrological calendar for the best days of the month for planting, and begin to plant outdoors.

୫ Set aside plenty of time to accomplish your list. Get children involved in the planting, too. It should be a family venture.

"I begin to reflect on nature's eagerness to sow life everywhere, to fill the planet with it, to crowd with it the earth, the air and the seas. Into every empty corner, into all forgotten things and nooks, nature struggles to pour life, pouring life into the dead, life into life itself. That immense overwhelming, relentless burning ardency of nature for the stir of life!"

—Henry Beston

May, the merriest month of the year, arrives bringing with it sunshine, singing birds, apple blossoms, budding lilacs and longer days to enjoy life as spring's promise is finally fulfilled. The month of May is named after the Greek goddess, Maia. She was the symbol of the Queen of the May, a young girl who stood for the rites of spring, the new growing season—the fertile soil.

May Day

May brings with it the hustle and bustle of many anxious gardeners rushing to start new life out in their gardens. It begins with a very special day, May Day, May 1.

May Day, the very merriest of festivals, is celebrated throughout Europe to awaken the gardens and flowers from the long winter's nap. During the Middle Ages in England, the May Day celebrations were characterized by May poles decorated with colorful ribbons and flowers, bonfires to drive away the ghosts of winter and people running through the woods to awaken the garden fairies.

On May Day's eve, people would wander through the woods, returning at daybreak with all the flowers that they had gathered to decorate their homes, May poles and May baskets.

Creeping out at dawn to secretly hang May Day baskets on the doors of fellow gardeners gives a wonderful feeling of being a part of an ancient tradition. Because May weather is often most uncooperative, it certainly can be a challenge to collect enough flowers for May baskets. Still a search of your garden and the fields is well worth the effort; scented geraniums, tulips, crocus, narcissus, daffodils, lilac and irises are a few of the flowers that may be in bloom.

May Day is a time to share your herb plants. It's a time to pass along cuttings, root divisions and plants to friends and neighbors. Herbing is sharing.

May Day is about old plants, new plants; old people, young people; shared plants, shared experiences, feeling, memories, opinions. Therefore, it is the ideal time to pass along some of your heirloom plants, those plants that are difficult to find anymore. These horticultural treasures are called "pass along plants" because

---

——— ॐ ———

After the uncertainties of April weather, no month is more warmly welcome than May.

Chaucer once wrote, "May with all thy floures and they greene, welcome be though fairies, freshe May."

May poles, May wine and May baskets signify the hope and joy of spring and sound the bells for the new growing season.

the only way to obtain them is to beg a piece or two from a sympathetic gardening friend. Luckily, to a gardener, all other gardeners are friends.

Other special plants to be included in your May Day baskets are ones that can not be started or propagated easily. These are plants that can not be started from seed and must be propagated by cuttings or root divisions. Some herb plants that you may enjoy giving or receiving are French tarragon, lemon verbena, pineapple sage, rosemary and scented geraniums. Sweet woodruff, long associated with flavoring May wine in Germany, is an especially appropriate plant to give on May Day. It grows as an attractive ground cover in the shade, and in May and June it flowers with dainty white beauties against its shiny green leaves. Interestingly, it takes on a wonderful aroma of fresh cut hay and vanilla as it dries.

Join the green spirits that herald the start of the new growing season. Decorate a tree on your front lawn with colorful ribbons to signify a May pole and invite friends and neighbors to celebrate May Day with May wine and to exchange May baskets.

Mother's Day

Have you ever wondered why Mother's Day is celebrated in the month of May, the beginning of the gardening season? Could it be that mothers have been given the responsibility of being the caretaker of the beauty and edible pleasure of God's gardens? This old world proverb completes this special day: "God could not be everywhere, so he created mothers."

Mothers have that special way of caring for plants in the garden in the same way in which they nurture their children. Patience. Encouragement. Protection. Knowledge. Care. It is interesting that the same qualities apply to being a good mother and a good gardener.

Planting the Garden

One of the things that should not be underplayed prior to planting is preparation of the soil. As was covered on page 78, some nutrients may need to be added based upon your soil test. It is also important to turn the soil to loosen it up as well as to get fresh oxygen and air mixed in. Spring is also a good time to add aged compost and manure into your soil to get the plants off to a good start.

When planting young plants, it is a good practice to water them immediately with a fertilized mixture. This prevents the young plants from going into transplant shock.

The hardiest of herbs can be planted when the temperature stays in the 40s, which can be as early as mid-April. Herbs such as chives, Greek oregano, lovage, sage and thyme can be planted at this time.

Depending on your location in the Midwest (see the hardiness zones on page 55), you can start planting your young transplants about May 1. This would include hardy perennials such as anise hyssop, chives, Greek oregano, French sorrel, French tarragon, lavender, lovage, all mints, sage, thyme and winter savory.

As the air and soil temperatures begin to warm to 55 to 60 degrees, sometime between May 1 and 15, herbs such as borage, chervil, cilantro, dill, parsley, purslane, summer savory and sweet marjoram can all be planted in the ground.

The tender perennial category of herbs, which includes lemon grass, lemon verbena, pineapple sage, myrtle, rosemary and all scented geraniums, can go outdoors but must be kept in pots so they can be brought indoors for the winter. The gardener can either plant tender perennials in decorative pots to be placed around the patio, deck or walkway, or plant them in plastic pots with drainage holes to be sunk directly into the ground. In early September, the pots can be dug up, washed off and brought in.

It is very important to start and grow your tender perennials in pots, transplanting them into larger pots as needed. They will grow and thrive much better than if planted in the ground and dug up at season's end to be put in pots. This disturbs the plants' roots, sometimes causing the plants to go into shock from which they may not recover.

If you have the space, two sets of tender perennials can be planted: one in a pot to be brought indoors and another in the ground to die off in winter.

ॐ

According to the Farmer's Almanac, the last date for frost in the Midwest is around May 20 each year. That means that one can not plant what's termed tender perennials and certain tender annuals prior to that date without some chance of losing to bad weather.

90

The last of the herbs to be planted is basil. This very tender annual dislikes cold, wet, damp weather and will thrive in warm soil when it is planted outdoors around Memorial Day. It is best to keep it in a pot indoors by a sunny window and transplant it when the soil has warmed up to 60 degrees. Basil, like tomatoes, needs warm soil and some protection in order to get established in the ground. If you want to take chances planting the many varieties of basil earlier in May, you will likely be replanting it again at May's end. It's best to wait to plant basil.

Now that we have discussed the general time frames of when to plant certain groups of herbs, we need to go back to our original gardening plans and the interrelationships of plants—companion planting.

Companion Planting

This season, pest-proof your garden by interplanting herbs among your vegetables and flowers. Companion gardening is an excellent and sometimes complete form of pest control. It discourages pests from massing repeatedly in one area, and along with crop rotation, it prevents the soil from becoming depleted of nutrients.

Interspersing or bordering certain aromatic herbs in vegetable, fruit and flower beds is a very effective pest-repelling tool for all gardeners. Naturally-resistant plants deter a variety of parasites from approaching their more vulnerable neighbors, either by camouflaging the alluring odor of a nearby plant or by repelling pests with the smell of the herb itself.

Some herbs you may want to interplant in your garden:

Anise: This is a good general repellent against aphids. From seed, it will germinate more quickly and thrive when sown near cilantro, which benefits from anise's presence. However, anise has a tendency to stunt the growth of carrots when planted too close.

Basil: It is a helpful stimulator of many vegetables including asparagus, eggplant and peppers and improves the taste and size of tomatoes. Sweet basil repels whiteflies as well as houseflies. It is an excellent herb to grow near the house to deter entry of these pests. Sprigs of the dried herb can also be hung around the door and window frames to further deter flies. Basil and rue should be planted far apart since they do not do well as neighbors.

Borage: Also known as "bee bread," this herb will attract beneficial insects to the garden as soon as their colorful flowers appear. It is best planted next to strawberries to stimulate each other's growth. Borage also complements squash and tomatoes while repelling tomato worms.

Catnip: This herb attracts bees to the garden. It also attracts cats, of course, and must be planted where they can't dig up entire beds to get at it. Catnip strongly repels a variety of garden pests and therefore protects many vegetables. Although catnip is very beneficial, it is best planted in pots and placed in the garden. Catnip draws nutrients from the soil, resulting in poor growth in surrounding crops. Its invasive roots will choke the the growth of other plants if allowed too much freedom.

Chamomile: Beneficial insects such as hover flies, who devour aphids on neighboring plants, are attracted to this herb. Chamomile can significantly improve the flavor and size of onions, cabbage and cucumbers. It also tends to increase the essential oil content of nearby aromatic herbs.

Chives and Garlic Chives: They are particularly noted for helping produce delicious and healthy carrots. Chives are great companions for tomatoes, roses, grapes and other fruit shrubs and trees. It has been found that peas and beans don't do well near chives. Tea-spray made from chives removes mildew and is an excellent pest repellent.

Dill: It is particularly beneficial to the cabbage family and improves the flavor and size of cucumbers, onions, corn and lettuce. As a member of the carrot family, and therefore susceptible to the same root diseases as carrots, dill should not be planted near carrots.

❧

*"First April,
she with mellow
showers, opens the
way for early
flowers.
Then after her
comes smiling May
In a more rich and
sweet array."*

—*Robert Herrick*

Garlic: Garlic is an excellent general repellent, especially of aphids. This plant has long been a favorite of rose growers. When garlic is planted close to rose bushes, it consistently protects them from black spot and other diseases. When planted throughout vegetables, it protects them from a host of insect assaults. But beware—it has a tendency to stunt the growth of peas and beans.

Hyssop: This herb has gained a certain reputation for its positive effects on the cabbage family, repelling white cabbage butterflies and also increasing the yield of vine crops. Hyssop is a gentle, non-invasive herb that has many uses in the vegetable garden. Planted near bean crops, it repels black flies while increasing the flavor and size of beans.

Lavender: This attractive lurer of bees and butterflies also has a positive effect on vegetables and other herbs, particularly thyme. Being aromatic, it deters many pests, notably and traditionally moths—both in the garden and when dried in the closet.

Marigolds (African and French): For centuries many gardeners have practiced just one form of companion/repellent planting for flower and vegetable crops—setting marigolds as hedging plants around beds. Marigold roots kill harmful nematodes in the soil and their flowering parts emit a range of delicate, repellent odors to parasites.

Marigolds can be planted just about anywhere they're needed, such as near beans, corn, melon, potatoes, squash and tomatoes. They're also beneficial to vulnerable flowers such as roses and tulips.

Marjoram: When interspersed throughout the garden, this herb will enhance the flavor of many vegetables, and when in flower, attract bees and butterflies. If stinging nettle is planted nearby, the essential oil content of marjoram becomes markedly increased. It also thrives in the company of sage.

ʒ

The Greeks planted marjoram on graves in order to help the dead sleep happily.

93

————— ॐ —————

*"To everything
there is a season,
and a time to every
purpose under
heaven;
A time to be born,
and a time to die;
A time to plant,
and a time to pluck
up that which is
planted."*

—Ecclesiastes

Mints: This excellent general repellent to ants, black flea beetles and cabbage caterpillars is traditionally set near cabbage family members. Since it is somewhat repellent to aphids, it will also help protect roses. Mints are good companions to tomatoes. Remember to plant in a pot in the ground to contain mint's invasive roots.

Nasturtiums: This flower attracts hover flies, which eat aphids on neighboring plants and fruit trees. Nasturtiums deter squash bugs and pumpkin beetles and also help melons and cucumbers. It improves the flavor and growth of radishes and beans.

Parsley: While minimally repellent to parasites, it is a great flavor enhancer of tomatoes and many gardeners find it also improves the growth and aroma of roses.

Rosemary: This herb and sage make excellent partners and stimulate each other's growth and flavor. Rosemary is very repellent to carrot flies and has a protective and flavor-enhancing effect on other vegetable crops such as beans and cabbage family members.

Rue: Mutually negative to basil, sage and cabbage, rue is best planted as a hedge or border for its strong aroma.

Sage: This herb is good to plant with marjoram and rosemary. It also improves the flavor of cabbage, carrots, tomatoes and strawberries. Do not plant near onions.

Savory: Summer savory, and to a lesser extent, winter savory, is noted for improving the quality of nearby onions. Both have a positive effect on the flavor of beans and helps deter bean beetles.

Southernwood: An excellent general repelling aid, it should be interspersed throughout the garden. This herb is one of the strongest moth repellents.

Tansy: Another excellent general repellent, tansy works well against small flying garden pests and ants. Plant near roses and fruit bushes and trees. Squash and cucumber react positively, but some say collards wilt when tansy is nearby.

Thyme: Like many other aromatic herbs, thyme improves the flavor of neighboring plants and acts as a strong deterrent to certain pests, especially cabbage worms. While in bloom, this herb is a favorite of bees.

Wormwood: Many gardeners find that this extremely aromatic herb inhibits the growth of, and may even be toxic to, neighboring plants. However, set around fences or perimeters of gardens, it can be useful to repel a variety of pests including slugs, snails, rodents and certain small animals. It also repels garden and clothes moths.

Yarrow: It heightens the flavor and taste of neighboring plants, especially herbs, and is noted for significantly increasing the essential oil production of aromatic herbs. Yarrow is also very enticing to a variety of beneficial insects including hover flies and ladybugs.

Astrological Gardening

Astrology is the study and use of the forces of nature as an aid in obtaining the highest possible degree of success, a tool to be used along with other helpful advice and information. In astrology, the moon is a symbol of the life-force, the reproductive energy that animates all living things—plants, animals and even human beings. Organic gardening teaches us how to plant in harmony with nature; astrology teaches us when.

Moon Planting

Those of us who practice moon planting believe we are working in harmony with nature's rhythms. We use the moon to help determine when it's best to sow and reap, believing that despite the vastness of our galaxy, the sun, moon and planets, stars and the earth are all in tune.

In order to plant your garden by the phases of the moon, you will need a good astrological calendar, such as Stella Natura (see page 234 for Resource Guide), which includes the daily zodiac signs. An annual almanac is needed as well.

It isn't necessary to understand why moon planting works; all that gardeners are interested in is the fact that it does work. So here it is simply stated.

When the moon is waxing, life-energy on earth increases; when it is waning, life-energy on earth decreases. As we embark on the major task of planting the garden, it is of utmost importance to plant when the life-energy on earth increases.

In general, during the increasing light from the new moon to full moon, plant annuals that produce their yield above the ground. An annual is a plant that completes its entire life cycle within one growing season and has to be seeded anew each year. Most vegetables are annuals.

During the decreasing light from the full moon to new moon, plant biennials, perennials and bulb and root plants. Biennials include crops that are planted one season to winter over and produce crops the next. Perennials and bulb root plants include all plants that grow from the same root year after year.

A simple, though less accurate rule, is to plant crops that produce above the ground during the increase of the moon and to plant crops that produce below ground during the decrease of the moon.

Here are some suggestions for using the correct quarters of the moon for gardening:

New Moon—beginning of the first quarter. Plant asparagus, barley, broccoli, brussels sprouts, cabbage, corn, cress, cucumbers, endive, kohlrabi, leeks, lettuce, oats, onions, parsley, spinach and seeds of herbs and flowering plants. Avoid the first day of the new moon for planting, also the days on which it changes quarters.

Second quarter—Plant beans, eggplant, muskmelons, peas, peppers, pumpkins, squash, tomatoes and watermelon. In both the first and second quarters it is best to plant seeds while the moon is in the fruitful signs of Cancer, Scorpio or Pisces. The next best signs are Taurus and Capricorn. For flowers, use Libra. For flowering vines, use Virgo. Onion and garlic seeds may be planted in Sagittarius.

——— ✿ ———

"But from flowers to stars, is the distance so great? If one stands beside them in the garden in the clear obscure of twilight, and watches the heavenly lights appearing faintly in the darkening sky, an inner feeling recognizes that they belong to the same world of influences and that we are one with them both."

—Candace Wheeler

Full Moon—beginning of the third quarter. Plant artichoke, beets, carrots, chicory, parsnips, potatoes, radishes, rutabaga, turnips and all bulbous flowering plants. Good also for planting biennials, perennials, onion sets, peanut, sage, strawberries, sunflowers, tubers for seed, apple trees, beech trees, deciduous trees, maple trees, oak trees, peach trees, pear trees, and plum trees.

Fourth quarter—During the fourth or last quarter of the moon. Turn sod, pull weeds and destroy unwanted growths, especially when the moon is in the barren signs of Gemini, Leo or Virgo. Not considered a good planting time, but possible for planting onion sets and sunflower seeds with some hope for success.

Successful lunar gardening should also include using your own common sense. Obviously, if you're having a blizzard when the moon's position indicates the planting of flowers, it is not a good time to plant. The correct lunar position can not compensate for weather conditions. Weather, season, temperature and your own personal schedule must also affect your gardening activities.

Gardener's Guide to the Zodiac

Just as each month of the year is dominated by one of the zodiac signs, so is each day of the month, as the moon moves through the different zodiac signs. Each sign will appear at least once a month for two or three days, and each is useful for some specific gardening practices.

The meanings of the zodiac signs within each month are:

Aries—Harvest, weed or cultivate.

Taurus—A feminine sign, moist and earthly; good for sturdy growth.

Gemini—A good sign to harvest, chop and weed.

Cancer—A watery and fruitful sign. Good for planting or transplanting.

Leo—Fiery, barren and dry, but good for harvesting.

Virgo—A rather dry but earthy sign, good for planting vines. Produces many blossoms but little fruit.

Libra—A lovely sign for flowers, airy and moist.

Scorpio—Good planting sign for seed or nursery stock.

Sagittarius—Good sign for weeding or cultivating.

Capricorn—Earthly, moist and feminine. A good "second best" sign.

Aquarius—Masculine, airy, barren and dry. Good for cultivation.

Pisces—Good for both planting and irrigation, a very fruitful sign.

For those who garden astrologically and organically, their activities are both therapeutic and joyful, a part of the ongoing journey toward spiritual awareness of becoming one with the earth.

Garden Notes:

JUNE

June To Do's

❧ Plant the balance of your garden, including basil, other kitchen herbs and strawberry jars.

❧ Water daily all newly-planted transplants for several weeks until plants are established. Water potted plants frequently as well.

❧ Enjoy your herb flowers in vinegars, salads and as a garnish, too.

"I have always thought a kitchen garden a more pleasant sight than the finest orangery…I love to see everything in perfection, and am more pleased to survey my rows of coleworts and cabbages, with a thousand nameless pot herbs springing up in their full fragrancy and verdure, than to see the tender plants of foreign countries."

—Joseph Addison

The Summer Solstice occurs in the northern hemisphere on June 20 or 21 and marks the official beginning of summer in the top half of the world. The word solstice comes from the Latin "solstitium," which translates as "sun standing still."

Once the sun has reached its peak at the solstice, the situation reverses and it moves slightly farther south every day, resulting in increasingly fewer hours of sunlight. It is logical to conclude that the June solstice, which many cultures celebrate as the first day of summer, is in fact the middle of summer, since it is the point at which the sun is highest and remains longest in the sky.

Nonetheless, in northern regions it is natural to think of the solstice as the beginning of the season because the hot weather of summer usually follows a few weeks afterwards (the lag is caused by the insulating effect of the surface of the earth that holds winter's cold even after the sun's warmth has increased).

The day of solstice begins slightly earlier than the day that precedes it and ends slightly later. It is a day-lovers delight: the longest day and shortest night of the year. But celebrations of the Summer Solstice are tempered with a bittersweet irony. The day following the solstice begins a bit later and ends a bit sooner; and the march toward winter begins.

Up until June 21, the airy, barren, dry and masculine sign of Gemini rules. This is the best time for pulling weeds, destroying noxious growths and trimming sod, especially during the fourth or last quarter of the moon. Zodiac gardeners believe that Cancer (June 21 to July 22) is the most productive sign of all for planting.

As we begin the month of June, our outdoor garden should begin to take shape with new plants getting established and showing signs of growth. By this time of the year, your indoor potted herbs should be moved outdoors, too. This is an ideal time to repot them into larger pots or divide them for more root space. For the plants that will later come indoors, it's best to always keep them in pots for less transplant shock. If you choose, you can transplant the larger potted plants into your garden and start new plants that can come indoors in September.

Now is the time to get the garden planted and established in order to have a wealth of herbs to be used in the kitchen all summer long.

Midsummer Eve was celebrated on June 23, the eve of the nativity of St. John the Baptist, and was said to be the witch's Sabbath, when evil could fall upon the season's crops in the critical few weeks before harvest. To protect the crops and throw some sympathetic magic toward the diminishing sun, bonfires were lit and the smoke from torches was allowed to drift downward over the fields.

Planting the Kitchen Garden

Today, more and more people are concerned about eating healthy, fresh foods and using less salt. When you grow and cook with herbs, you will be adding that special bit of magic and flavor—that special surprise that awakens your taste buds. Fresh herbs spark your palate, add many new and exciting flavors without calories, salt or fats. All natural, all flavorful!

A kitchen herb garden should contain most of the herbs that you would normally use in cooking. There are 12 basic culinary herbs that are recommended for a starter herb garden. You may want to add or subtract from the list. These are the basic plants and the number of each for a garden 20 feet deep and 15 feet wide:

1 or 2 chive plants

3 to 6 (or more) basil plants

2 rosemary plants

1 sage plant

3 Greek oregano plants

3 sweet marjoram plants

6 Italian parsley plants

3 French tarragon plants

3 thyme plants

1 or 2 savory plants

2 or 3 dill plants

1 or 2 mint plants

Before you finalize your list of herb plants, check with your cookbooks to see if you'd like to add something unusual like pineapple sage (tender perennial), lemon verbena (tender perennial) or anise hyssop (perennial).

When planting your first herb garden, it's best to start with plants, not seeds, in order to get them established early in the growing season.

Sample Kitchen Herb Garden

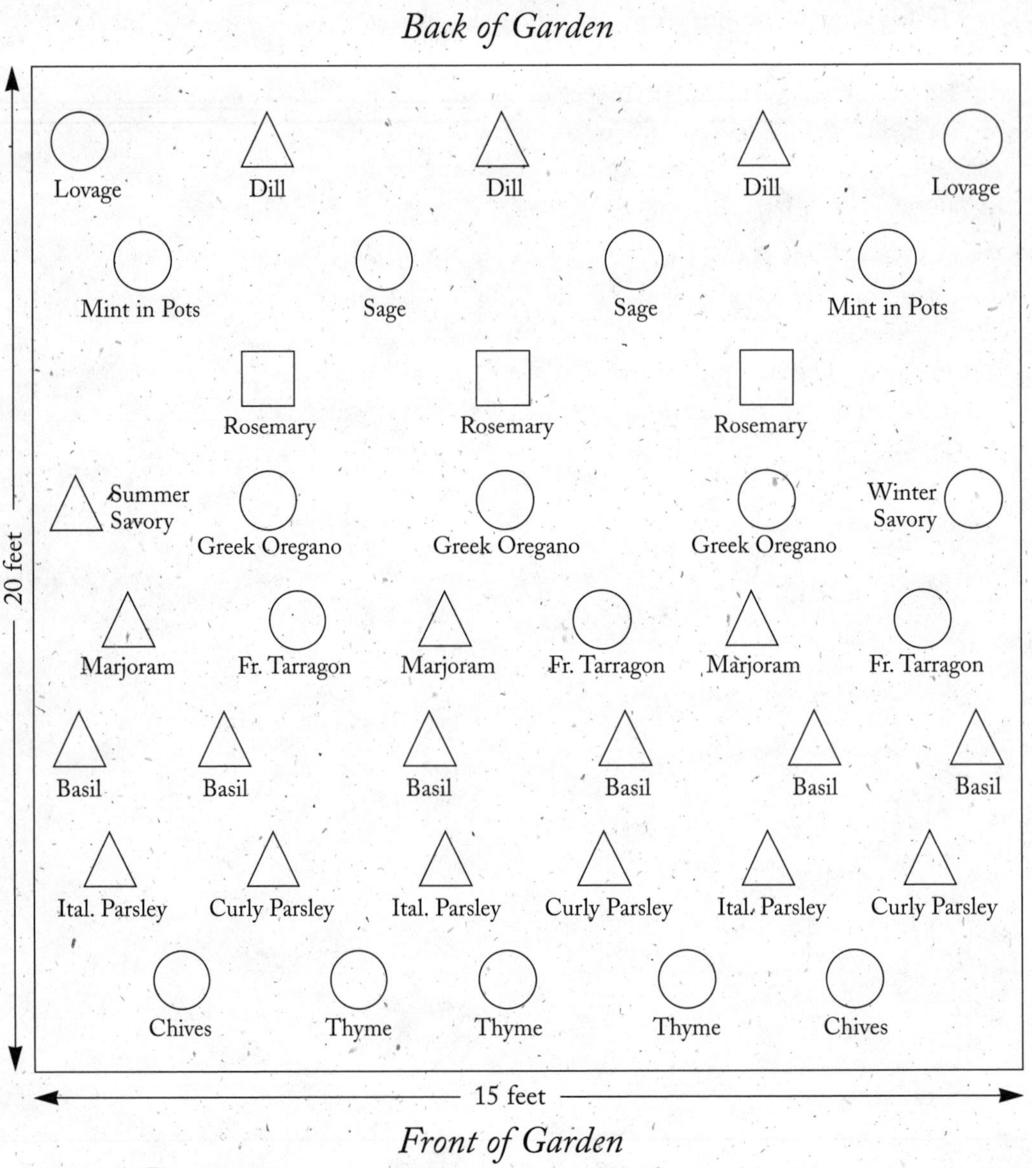

Back of Garden

○ Lovage	△ Dill	△ Dill	△ Dill	○ Lovage
○ Mint in Pots	○ Sage	○ Sage	○ Mint in Pots	
□ Rosemary	□ Rosemary	□ Rosemary		
△ Summer Savory	○ Greek Oregano	○ Greek Oregano	○ Greek Oregano	○ Winter Savory
△ Marjoram	○ Fr. Tarragon	△ Marjoram	○ Fr. Tarragon	△ Marjoram ○ Fr. Tarragon
△ Basil	△ Basil	△ Basil	△ Basil	△ Basil △ Basil
△ Ital. Parsley	△ Curly Parsley	△ Ital. Parsley	△ Curly Parsley	△ Ital. Parsley △ Curly Parsley
○ Chives	○ Thyme	○ Thyme	○ Thyme	○ Chives

20 feet

15 feet

Front of Garden

○ Hardy Perennials—plant in permanent spot

□ Annuals—to be planted each year

△ Tender Perennials—plant in pots; sink in ground; dig up in September; and bring indoors for winter

These plants can be grown in the ground or in containers—the choice is yours. The end result is the same; plenty of fresh herbs to use in cooking.

Try to locate the garden close to the kitchen so that it is easy to go out and get your daily snippets to use. As a general rule, most herbs prefer full sun for good growth and flavor. Be sure to select the proper location for your herb garden. Consult Herbs in Profile, pages 3-52, for more details on specific requirements of growing individual herb plants.

Herbs are undemanding plants that like a slightly acidic soil (5.5 to 6.5 pH), and for the most part, once the plants are established, they prefer to be dry rather than too moist.

Most herbs can be planted from mid-May forward, with the exception of basil. It needs 60-degree days and nights, so it's best to plant basil toward the end of May or early June.

At this half-way point in the garden, it's a good time to groom and trim, and still put in new plants. I prefer to plant in stages instead of all at once. When moving plants started in pots to the garden, soak the plant in its pot in a bucket of fertilized water. Then plant the pot in the soil. This will get the plant off to a good start. Perennials added to your garden at this time will be firmly established before fall and winter.

Planting in Strawberry Jars

Not everyone has the right conditions to grow culinary herbs in the ground. For those with limited outdoor space or a great deal of shade in the garden, growing herbs in a strawberry jar is an alternative to growing them in the ground. Much pleasure can be derived from cultivating a strawberry jar of herbs. The plants and container take up little room and are delightful to look at. Harvesting the herbs for cooking is a deliciously rewarding bonus.

Remember that when growing in containers, you must water the plants more often.

A strawberry jar is just one way of growing several herbs in one pot. Depending on the space you may have, you can create a whole garden in pots. Container gardening has become a popular option to gardening in the ground—the choice is yours (see page 163 for details on strawberry jars and container gardening).

Watering

There are three things that your garden needs. First your garden needs sun, which we can not control, but only make the most of. Secondly, it needs soil, which we can enrich with products such as fertilizer, food and mulch. Thirdly, it needs water.

It is the most unusual of circumstances when nature provides enough of it in our surroundings, so water becomes a fundamental need. Even if you have the most sophisticated irrigation and sprinkling system known to modern man, you still need a good old pliable hose long enough to reach anywhere on the property that you are likely to plant.

Depending on the size of your garden, you may want to water daily, preferably when the heat of the day subsides, usually about two hours before sunset during the summer. A late afternoon watering will wash off the dust, grime and insects from the plant leaves. By watering late in the afternoon with a hand sprayer, you also allow the water to penetrate into the soil for a half day or more before the sun and wind reappear in strength. When they do, the bed will be a good reservoir of water from which the plants can draw. The cool water is warmed by the warm soil and the temperature is modified by the time it reaches the plant roots. The roots suffer less shock because they are being watered with warm instead of cold water. Watering in late afternoon is a good idea, too, because the plants actually do a significant amount of their growing at night.

If you water early in the morning, much of the water will be lost to evaporation caused by the sun and wind. The water loss will be even greater if you water at mid-day. If you water in the evening, the plants will be more susceptible to mildew and rust problems due to the unevaporated water left on the leaves.

A system of timed soaker hoses will alleviate the problem of wet leaves and will send the water right down to the roots of your plants, thus watering the plants, not the surrounding weeds. This procedure will allow a thorough soaking once a week during extremely dry conditions.

Be aware that you must adjust your watering according to the weather. A plant bed may lose more moisture on a cloudy,

In summer the days seem to stretch out forever. It is a season of abundant life. "The dog days of summer" are tainted with the knowledge that they will soon be growing shorter and the nights longer. Ancient beliefs tell us that during the hottest part of summer, dragons patrolled the sky and witches were active.

windy, dry day than on a hot, clear, humid and still one. There are times when the beds need no water (after a heavy rainfall) or may need watering twice a day (during hot, dry spells).

One way to determine whether you have watered enough is to go out the next morning and poke your finger into the bed. If the soil is evenly moist for the first two inches and continues to be moist below this level, you are watering properly. If the soil is dry for part or all of the first two inches, you need more water.

When watering, you must consider the different nature of plants. Plants in containers or pots, especially clay pots, have a tendency to dry out more quickly than plants in the garden, and therefore, need more water.

Established, hardy perennials have greater stamina to withstand a drought period than younger plants and annuals that will need to be watered more frequently. Young seedlings and immature plants growing in beds will need to be watered morning, noon and later afternoon for a total of at least an inch of water a week. Later when the living mulch occurs, that is, when the leaves grow closer together, less watering will be required.

Be sure to water the sides and edges of the planting beds more frequently because they have a tendency to dry out faster than the center beds. These areas, which many people miss or underemphasize, are critical because they are subject to more evaporation. Pay special attention to older beds; because the root system is thicker, several waterings may be required to get the proper penetration.

Similarly, newly-dug but still unplanted beds should be watered daily so they will not lose their moisture content. A transplant in a bed that has a low moisture level will have difficulty growing well because of the dry soil below.

The heat, as well as the strength of the sun can kill, so be keenly aware of your plants— especially when leaves begin to curl and droop.

When the sun is hot and temperatures get above 85 degrees, plants droop slightly; the leaves bend somewhat and the plants do not stand erect. The plants are just minimizing the water loss. Watering them at this time will increase water loss rather than lessen it and weaken the plant through too much pampering. It is best to wait until later in the afternoon to water, preferably with a soaker hose to get the the roots quickly.

A more extreme case of drooping occurs when the plants have actually weakened from lack of water. These plants will hang over and seem lifeless. The upper part of the plants will hang and the leaves will curl inward. Plants in this state will revive, but they will have suffered some permanent damage—an open invitation for pests and diseases.

Eventually, the watering process will become automatic and you will not even have to think about when the bed has received enough water.

Be sure to realize you are watering the soil, not the plant directly. Keeping the soil alive will retain water best and minimize the water consumed. Soil that is rich in compost and humus will retain water and in the long run will not need to be watered as frequently.

Harvesting Herb Flowers

By mid-June your garden should be well underway and the plants should be showing signs of new growth. When the plants are about eight inches tall, you can begin to cut or harvest them so that they will also bush out. Always cut the stem above another set of leaves with garden shears.

Let's talk about allowing your herb plants to flower. I am one in a million who strongly believes in allowing my herb plants to flower. Most herb growers believe that once herbs flower, the flavor of the herb is less potent. In my opinion there is such a minimal change in flavor it's not enough to be concerned about. Gardening should be fun; we should enjoy the many changes that our plants go through. Flowers are a way of showing us that the plants are happy and thriving, and for some herbs, flowering is the start of new growth.

All herb flowers should be harvested early to mid morning, just after the dew has dried and before full sun. Place flowers in the refrigerator to keep cool until ready to use. All herb flowers are edible. They range in flavor from bland to spicy, sweet to piquant.

Many can be eaten raw, while others need to be cooked. Flowers differ from all other ingredients in the impact they can

Sprinkling yourself with fern seed on Midsummer's Eve could make you invisible. If you walked backward that night and caught a branch of hazel from between your knees it would lead you to hidden treasure. To test the branch's potency, hold it near water. If it squeals like a pig, it is highly charged stuff.

make because they add a totally new dimension to cooking—that of color.

The possibilities for using edible flowers in cooking are limited only by your imagination and flavor preference. It's fun to make candied flowers to decorate cakes and sandwiches, flower butters, flower honeys, flower sugars, flower syrup, flower jellies, flower oils, flower vinegars, flower dips and flower spreads.

Chives and their other allium relatives, for example, are hardy perennials with grasslike leaves and beautiful flowers that are very attractive in the garden. Don't be deceived by their delicate beauty, their flowers are quite flavorful with an oniony punch. When using the flower in cooking, it is best to break it into individual florets so that it's not so pungent. This is the only time of the year to make chive blossom vinegar (see page 181 for information on making herb vinegars). It looks great in the bottle and tastes great, too. The blossoms can be added to fresh cooked asparagus and sesame seeds, gazpacho, Oriental stir frys, tossed with new potatoes, chicken salad and included on your favorite coleslaw recipe or garden salad.

When plants are in full bloom, cut the entire plant straight across to encourage more growth of chive stems.

Garlic chives bloom in late August or early September with a lacy white flower to be used in cooking, bouquets and wreaths.

Mints and their flowers make wonderful mint chocolate cakes, ice creams or sauces for desserts. Try adding mints to fruit salads and Tabbouleh.

Sage flowers in midsummer; its beautiful purple flowers have a milder flavor than the leaves. The flowers appear in whirls with lipped corollas that are outstanding. Some of the culinary treats that can be made from the flowers include sage fritters, sage pesto, orange, fennel and sage salad, and a sage crusted lemon sole.

Rosemary usually flowers indoors anywhere from December through March, but some types will flower in July and August. It must flower to start its new growth. The flowers can be used to make jellies and vinegars, or it can be sprinkled on salads.

Basil—The Exception

The family of basils are the only herbs that should not be allowed to flower. Basil will stop producing leaves after it flowers. The flower should be cut off before it gets to one inch tall. If you harvest the upper florets of basil, nipping off the white flowers as you do so, you are already preventing the plant from flowering.

Cinnamon basil can be allowed to flower, however, because its aroma is intoxicating. The flower can be cut off continually for garnishing, and cinnamon basil makes a great herb jelly for basting roasts.

Diatomaceous Earth

Once your garden is fully planted, it's a good idea to walk through your garden daily checking for insect holes on the leaves of herbs. For whatever reason, little black flea beetles love to make holes in the spicy leaves. Dusting the plants with Diatomaceous Earth will lessen their population. DE works on slugs and any other soft-bodied bugs as well. It is made from ground oyster shells, so that when insects rub against the powder they get cut, lose their body fluids and die.

Garden Notes:

ॐ

To the Hindus of India, sacred basil is the most sacred of all plants and is planted on graves and around temples as well as in the home. It is thought to be a protection against evil and every Hindu is buried with a basil leaf on his breast.

JULY

July To Do's

❧ Keep garden well watered. Mulch and side dress with organic materials to retain moisture in soil and fertilizer.

❧ Encourage birds, bees, butterflies and toads to visit your garden.

❧ Spray and dust your plants with natural pesticides.

❧ Use herbs to keep pests away from family and pets.

❧ Fertilize soil organically.

❧ Have an herbal "tea" party for all the plants in your garden.

"The kiss of the sun for pardon,
The song of the birds for mirth,
One is nearer God's heart in a garden
Than anywhere else on earth."

—Dorothy Frances Gurney

Nature's Helpers

Bees, butterflies and birds are some of nature's helpers—the more you have around the garden, the fewer the insects. By gardening organically without chemicals and planting herbs and flowers that will attract them, you will send out invitations for all bees, butterflies and birds to come visit.

Bees

Bees are the only insects that provide man with food. The Romans believed that the best honey came from Mount Hymettus in Athens where the fields were covered with wild thyme. Early settlers brought the honey bee and herbs to North America in the 17th century and they have been very important to us ever since. Ninety percent of agricultural crops benefit from insect pollination and bees play an important role in the pollinating process.

Bees don't care what kind of neighborhood they are in as long as nectar and pollen are available. Once a worker bee finds a patch of flowers, they do a dance and invite their fellow bees to come and feast. Bees will travel several miles looking for nectar.

Bees are attracted by color more than by scent. They respond to more vibrant colors such as yellow, blue, blue-green, mauve, purple and red (containing ultraviolet). Planting flowers in bold groups and drifts attracts bees because they like to carry as much nectar as they can; bees seldom visit a solitary flower.

For a good supply of bees during the growing season, you'll need to have a continual supply of nectar. As spring unfolds, some of the first nectar is from fruit tree blossoms—apple, cherry, plum and pear. Some perennial herbs will flower at this time too: thymes, marjoram and sages. During the summer, lavender and catnip will attract bees, and the flowers of winter savory and hyssop will keep bees busy in the fall.

Other herbs and flowers that you can plant in your garden to attract bees to pollinate and to produce nectar for honey include: alfalfa, alyssum, anise hyssop, basil, bee balm, borage, chamomile, foxglove, garlic chives, horehound, lemon balm, marshmallow, mints, red clover, rosemary, savories, veronica, white turtlehead and yellow centaurea. Bees are also attracted to flowers such as daisies, globe thistles, meadowsweet, monarda, nasturtiums and poppies.

Bees play an important role in the garden, but with bees come the possibility of bee stings. There are some herbs in your garden that can be used to relieve the sting. They are calendula, lamb's ear, comfrey and hyssop. Steep about one-half cup of herbs in warm water; dip a cloth or cotton ball in the herbal solution and apply to sting.

Butterflies

There are over 700 species of butterflies, which fly during the day differing from moths which fly at night. Butterflies and moths differ from bees in that they are attracted to sources of nectar by scent. In fact, they are scented, and scent plays a direct part in their sexual attraction. Flowers that are fertilized by butterflies and moths usually have a heavy, sweet scent which is found in old-fashioned flowers such as honeysuckle, jasmine, lilacs, narcissus and wallflowers.

A butterfly garden is a great place in which a weary gardener can rest to watch the butterflies. Be sure to position a bench within the area. The garden should be placed out of the wind and in full sun, a quiet enclosed area for privacy, good for meditation and reading.

A butterfly garden should be chock-full of herbs and flowers, but do not include wormwood or southernwood as butterflies do not like their strong aromas. Certain butterflies prefer particular flowers. A Red Admiral needs nettles to breed in. Monarchs need the milkweed plant, with its fragrant pink flowers. A Swallowtail likes parsley, fennel, dill and anise. Fritillaries will visit violets. Painted Ladies like the thistle-type plants. Coppers feed on dock and sorrel.

Butterflies prefer a weedy area, so do minimal weeding in the butterfly garden. Make a butterfly puddle by scooping out an area and keeping it slightly muddy. Every now and then you may see one of their "drinking parties" in the puddle.

During all four of the butterfly's stages of life—egg, larva, pupa and the butterfly—it is very sensitive to chemicals. It will not go where chemicals have been used as sprays on plants. Therefore, it is the organic gardener who is blessed with the fluttering of butterflies in the garden.

Birds

Birds have always been associated with gardens. In the 1700s and 1800s aviaries were built near dining areas so that birds could serenade people as they dined. Not only are birds desirable for their song and beauty, but more importantly for their enormous appetite for insects. Barn swallows, as well as other birds, follow the insect population and eat insects as the main part of their diet. It's fun to watch them swooping down over the fields and ponds or creeks, scooping up insects.

In order to attract birds for insect control, we need to make the garden an attractive place for them to visit. There are three necessary requirements for enticing birds to your garden—food, water and shelter.

To keep birds in your garden during the summer, you should feed them during the hard, cold winter months. Some people prefer to feed them year-round. If you are starting a new feeding station, set it up now, in July or August, since it does take time for the word to get around that you are offering winter accommodations. The birds come to depend on you for their food supply, so once you start feeding them, don't stop!

A bird bath or water garden will provide the birds with their water supply. Continue to supply water daily in the winter, too. Shelter can be in the form of a birdhouse or hedgerows, trees and shrubs.

Fruit trees and berries are their favorite places to gather and feast. Flowers such as alyssum, anise hyssop, bee balm, columbine, coral bells, dahlia, foxglove, hollyhocks, nasturtiums, red salvia, sage and snapdragons will also attract them to your garden because they love the nectar.

They are good weather forecasters, so watch them. When it's about to rain birds fly about chirping. The moisture in the air makes them jittery, causing the birds to fly about in a nervous state.

Toads

Another beneficial creature to have in a garden is the toad. Toads are bug-eating machines and one of the few predators that eat slugs. It has been said that in three months a single toad will eat up to 10,000 insects and cutworms. They feed at night and hide during the day.

Toad houses can be made from cracked flowerpots turned upside down and sunk into the ground with an inch or so above ground. Break a hole at ground level for an entrance. Toads drink through their skin, so they must have a basin or pond near the garden.

Natural Pesticides for the Garden

As Oliver Wendell Holmes said: "On every stem on every leaf, and at the root of everything that grew, was a professional specialist in the shape of grub, caterpillar, aphids or other expert, whose business it was to devour that particular part." While there are many beneficial insects that we need to have in our gardens, we all get annoyed when the harmful bugs begin to defoliate and kill precious flowers and vegetables. How can we keep them under control?

During these summer months we must deal with the pests of the garden naturally for our own health as well as for the safety of our environment.

There is a strong movement toward using natural repellents against pests. Pests don't build up an immunity to natural, botanical repellents and insecticides. This is partly because some herbs emit powerful aromatic and volatile oils which are repulsive to many insects. Their sense of smell is more acute than ours, and these aromas are overwhelmingly unpleasant. Pests will promptly abandon a pet, person or area where such herbs—fresh, dried, powdered or in essential oil form—are in use. Certain herbs and other botanical materials also act as insecticides rather than repellents and are completely harmless to mammals and the environment.

Our challenge is to rid our plants of pests naturally. If hand-picking and mechanical methods don't work, you may need a dust or spray to get rid of them.

Dusting

Some insects can be controlled by feeding them to death. For example, if you dust plants threatened by Colorado potato beetles with dry wheat bran early in the morning, the beetles will eat the bran, drink the dew to satisfy their thirst and then later burst from the water-expanded bran.

Cornmeal can be used as a dust to control cutworms; they eat the cornmeal but can't metabolize it, and eventually it kills them. Some gardeners have found that a dusting of one part salt and two parts flour is fatal to the cabbage worm.

Cayenne pepper will burn and suffocate a number of pests such as caterpillars and cabbage and tomato worms. Dust it on leaves after a rain to adhere more firmly. Dried powder dusted along pathways will also greatly repel ants.

Spraying

Sometimes, on certain plants or with certain pests, a spray is better than dust. Sprays usually give a more even coverage. Depending on the size of your garden, sprayers are available from the hand-held mist type of model to the backpack model.

Bug juice is a spray made from crushed insect pests and applied to the infested plants. Bug juice may indeed be a good control because grinding up the insects could release their "alarm pheromone" or warning scent which frightens other bugs away.

To make bug juice, collect half a cup of the specific problem insect. Place the pests in a blender with two cups of lukewarm water, and liquefy them. Strain the liquid through cheesecloth or a fine sieve to prevent particles from clogging your sprayer. Dilute about one-quarter cup water of the strained liquid with one or two cups of water to be used in a small hand sprayer (the leftover liquid can be frozen for a year or more).

Spray both sides of your vegetable leaves along with the stems and runners. If it rains, spray again. For obvious reasons, don't use a household blender to make this juice! Use an old blender jar, or mash the insects up with a mortar and pestle and add water.

The fatty acid salts in liquid dish soaps and commercial insecticidal soaps kill a large percentage of common insect pests including aphids, mites and whiteflies. Don't confuse homemade kitchen soap sprays with commercial soap sprays. The commercial

Healthy soil and healthy plants will survive a bug attack. Success starts from the ground up, so be sure to rotate your crops annually to get rid of places where bugs might breed or overwinter.

brands have been especially formulated to be lethal to specific pests, and to avoid damage to plants and beneficial insects. Insecticidal soap is biodegradable within seven to 14 days and, for the most part, attacks only problem insects. It will not harm beneficial insects, animals or people.

Spray plants every two or three days for two weeks for bad infestations. This should be done on a cloudy day or later in the day, not when the sun is out in full force. Wet all parts of the plants including the underside of the leaves, where you'll find most of the pests. The spray must have direct contact with the insect to be effective. It is best to wash off the spray the next morning before the sun beats down on the plants; this will reopen the pores of the leaves.

Insecticidal soap is not good for edible flowers as they become spotted and discolored. For flowers, you can use a garlic spray, consisting of one tablespoon concentrated garlic juice or eight to ten chopped cloves per quart of water. After mixture stands overnight it can be sprayed on plants where it will keep most pests away. Garlic, onion and chive sprays are effective in controlling insects on other plants as well. They don't actually kill insects but discourage them from attacking the plants. Making onion or chive spray is similar to making garlic spray. Chop peeled onions or chives into fine particles. Mix one-half cup of ground-up material with one pint of water, then strain out the particles to form a clear solution.

There are some light horticultural oils that work as an insecticide when diluted with water by spraying a thin coating on leaves, thus suffocating soft-bodied, sucking insects. Follow directions on the container.

A hot pepper spray can also be an effective insect control. This spray can be made by chopping or grinding hot peppers into fine particles and mixing one-half cup of them with one pint of water. Shake well, allow to steep several hours and strain through cheesecloth into a spray applicator. Avoid getting this solution near your eyes. Hot pepper powder can also be used to make a spray.

And last, but certainly not least, is Sal Gilbertie's family remedy called "Nana's Bug Juice." Put a couple of cloves of garlic and some cayenne pepper in one-half cup of water or cider vinegar and pour into a blender. Mix ingredients thoroughly, pour through a cheesecloth to strain. Pour the liquid into a mister to spray on your plants.

Herbs as Insect Repellents for People and Pets

Just as we can protect our gardens from insects naturally, we can also protect ourselves and our pets. Pests such as fleas, lice, ticks, chiggers, mosquitoes and gnats can all be effectively controlled by using herbs in their fresh, dried or essential oil form.

Fresh and Dried Herbs

The strongest herbal repellents against pests on pets and humans are citronella, eucalyptus, pennyroyal, rosemary, rue and wormwood. Milder ones include basil, bay, lavender, sage and thyme. The leaves of such plants can simply be rubbed on pets and people to temporarily ward off insect attacks.

The fresh and dried plants can be used in other ways too. The citrosa scented geranium plant works to ward off pests when planted by the door entrances of the house. The fresh or dried leaves of rosemary or bay set in water on the grill or simply tossed into the fire will repel insects while emitting an appetizing aroma to everyone else. And dried leaves of pennyroyal, rosemary or wormwood can also be placed in small muslin bags and tucked into pockets for additional protection from biting insects.

Essential Oils

Essential oil is the strongest form of repellents. The effects of essential oils are longer-lasting and, like powdered herbs, are often more convenient for personal and pet applications and for incorporating into house-cleaning chores.

These potent concentrated plant extracts are not oily as the name implies. A few drops in a simmering pot of water will temporarily but thoroughly diffuse a pleasant scent throughout a particular area. Applied directly to pets, fleas become stunned and drop off the animal. They will avoid returning to that pet, at least while the pet exudes such a repulsive odor.

Basil has a traditional use as a strewing herb to keep away flies, and was also an ingredient in sweet washing waters.

A good starting point is to use one-half teaspoon of oil per pint of cool water. After experimenting, you may want to increase this measure to accommodate young animals, children and sensitive skin.

The most commonly available repellent oils are basil, bay, eucalyptus, lavender, pennyroyal, rosemary and thyme. Pennyroyal oil is the strongest overall repellent and is especially effective against ticks and chiggers. In its pure oil form, it can cause skin irritations and needs to be used only in its diluted form. The fresh, dried and powered forms of pennyroyal may, however, be used quite safely on all pets, including small and newborn ones.

Citronella, with its clean lemony scent, is one of the most popular and familiar repellents. While deterring most pests, it is particularly effective against gnats and mosquitoes. Dab some on propane and camp lights to deter pests.

Other Natural Insect Repellents and Ointments

Lemons are an excellent parasite repellent, insecticide and skin tonic for mange and other skin disorders. Applied locally to pets with ringworm patches, the juice dries into a coating that prevents the fungus mold from developing. Squeezed onto bee or other bites and stings, the juice draws out poisons and relieves itching. It works on people, too.

Health food stores and herbalists usually carry salves made with comfrey roots and aloe vera gel. These skin-healing ointments are extremely effective, often when nothing else works.

Many parasites will be killed off while repelling them through methods such as drowning and vacuuming. However, many more will probably survive, and if pets have outdoor or yard access, it could well be a constant battle to keep them free of pests. A step beyond the herbal repellents may be necessary if the outbreak is explosive and occurs in more than one room. In such circumstances, natural botanies such as Pyrethrum powders or Diatomaceous Earth are recommended. Both are nontoxic to mammals but lethal to insects—DE to all crawling insects and Pyrethrums to all crawling and flying ones. They may be safely applied inside and outside the home, as well as directly on pets.

Natural Fertilizers

In this time frame, you the gardener, must make an important choice—that of whether to use organic fertilizers or chemical fertilizers.

Prior to the 19th century the fertilizers that were used were humus and manure. Soil was considered simple chemistry—nitrogen, phosphorus and potash. In the 1920s, chemical fertilizers were seen as a quick-fix solution for poor soil. Chemicals do work in the short run. But lost in the shuffle is the fact that the soil is a living thing.

Overuse of chemical fertilizers can actually harm soil life. Chemical fertilizers tend to be more water soluble, leaching out the soil faster than the plant can use it. By using commercial fertilizers year after year without putting in organic matter, the soil is drained of valuable nutrients. Chemicals provide immediate nutrients but do nothing for the texture and structure of the soil in order to provide a favorable environment for important soil organisms.

Organic fertilizers are quite different from chemical fertilizers because they not only feed the plant, they also feed the soil. Organic fertilizers become part of the soil, working to release beneficial trace nutrients gradually as the plants need them. An application of an organic fertilizer at planting time reduces the need for several uses during the season.

A wide variety of materials that are found in nature can be used as organic fertilizers—aged manure, compost, soybean and cottonseed meal, seaweed, decomposed hay or straw, leaves and grass clippings. When you mulch or side dress with these materials, you are adding fertilizer to your garden.

Adding natural fertilizers makes your garden healthy. When your soil is healthy, diseases and insects are less likely to attack.

Herbal Fertilizer

July is a good time to have an herbal fertilizer "tea" party for your garden. There are many plants in your garden right now that you can use as "teas" to add nutrients to your soil. Here are some herbs and plants that will perform magic in your garden when used in teas.

Coltsfoot—provides sulphur and potassium

Couch grass—(a weed) rich in minerals, potassium and silica

Dill—rich in minerals, potassium, sulphur and sodium

Dandelion—good source of copper

Fat hen—contains iron and other materials

Fenugreek—sprouted seed heads are rich in both nitrates and calcium

Horsetail—high concentration of silica

Stinging nettle—a treasure house of silica, iron, nitrogen, minerals and trace elements

Sunflower—ash of stalks is high in potash

Tansy—rich in potassium and other minerals

Tea leaves—contains nitrogen, phosphoric acid, manganese and potash; these are locked in tannis but released by brewing

Yarrow—provides copper and a good general fertilizer

To make fertilizer teas, you don't have to buy a thing. Use this standard recipe for all herbal fertilizer teas: Pour four cups of boiling water over a handful of fresh herbs or two tablespoons of dried herbs. Cover and allow to infuse for 10 minutes, then strain herbs through cheesecloth before using the liquid.

Teas can be applied directly to the soil or sprayed on the leaves. If you are using the tea as a foliar spray, it's best to add one tablespoon of molasses per gallon of tea so that the spray will adhere to the leaves.

Application of foliar sprays are best done about an hour or two before sunset or after sunrise. Leaves are not receptive when the sun is hot and during the heat of mid-day. It's also best to

apply a foliar spray during times of stress, especially from pro-
longed dry, hot weather or when the plants look limp and under-
nourished. Another crucial time is when plants start to form buds,
blossoms, fruits and seeds.

Try giving your plants herbal teas and see the improvement
in flavor and quality and the extension of the fruiting season.

Garden Notes:

AUGUST

August To Do's

❧ Begin to harvest and preserve your herbs by drying or freezing.

❧ Make vinegars, oils, jellies and butters.

❧ Start your indoor garden plants.

"The enjoyments of a garden being so manifold and continuous, bringing brightness to the home, health to the body, and happiness to the mind, it is for us, who have proved them, whose daily lives are made more cheerful by their influence, out of our gratitude and our good will, to invite and to instruct others, that they may share our joy."

—S. Reynolds Holie

Here it is the month of August. The herbs in the garden are growing well and you've been using them fresh for cooking all summer. Soon the cold weather will be upon us and we need to begin to harvest, preserve and store the herbs for continued use all year long.

Harvesting

To enjoy the rewards of your garden, it is essential to harvest herbs properly. Herbs begin to wilt soon after cutting so it's best to put aside a whole day or some time each day for harvesting.

The best time to pick herbs is on a clear day, as soon as the dew evaporates but before the sun's heat dries up the essential oils. Mid-morning from 9:00 to 11:00 is the ideal time.

If you're harvesting herbs for fragrance, try to pick the plants just before they bloom, when they're at their most aromatic. If you're picking for flowers, pick them soon after the buds open, before the petals start to fade and brown.

Place cut plants, leaves and flowers gently in a flat-bottomed basket, English trug or wooden box. Keep the basket or box shaded while you harvest, to preserve the essential oils. Do not put plants in a sack or bag; this will crush and bruise the herbs and make them sweat.

Following are some suggestions for preserving your harvested herbs. There are other methods as well, so experiment and see what works best for you.

Always add fresh, frozen or dried herbs the last few minutes of cooking as they tend to lose their flavor. The only exception is bay leaves which become more fla-vorful during long periods of cooking.

Drying Herbs

Most of the aromatic herbs, like bay, rosemary, sage, thyme and winter savory, dry with as much flavor as they have when they are fresh.

Once leaves or flowers are cut from the stem, metabolic changes begin, cells start to die and medicinal values and flavors are reduced. The sooner drying begins, and the quicker the method, the better the quality and color of the dried herb.

After you've cut the herbs, wipe off any soil but avoid washing leaves unless it's absolutely necessary. Keep the leaves out of sunlight as this extracts essential oils.

Hanging To Dry

Here are two methods for hanging herbs to dry:

1. Gather up small bunches of herbs, tie with string or a rubber band and hang upside down.

2. Gather up small bunches as above. With leaves facing toward the ground, put in a small brown paper bag (lunch bag size). Gather the opening of the bag around the tied bunches, tie with string and hang "bagged herbs" from a line or peg. Be sure to punch holes in the bag. This method will keep a greener color to the leaves once dried. It'll also keep the dried herbs free from dust and dirt in the air.

Whichever method you use, hang the herbs in a warm dry, dark room with ventilation, such as an attic or basement, an old barn or drying shed. The herbs can be hung from beams or wall pegs. A drying temperature of 90 degrees is ideal for the first 24 hours with cooler temperatures thereafter. The faster they dry, the better for color and flavor.

When dry, remove leaves from stems. The best method is to hold the stem and slide your thumb and index finger down the stem, going from top to bottom. You may want to wear gloves to protect your hands from the dry twigs. Keep leaves whole so they retain their scent; break them up only if necessary to fit into jars. Leaves should be stored in an airtight glass bottle or jar away from sunlight, moisture and dust. Plastic and metal containers affect the herb's chemistry. Crush the leaves just before using.

Microwave Drying

Herbs can easily be dried in your microwave oven. This method speeds up the process of drying considerably and retains the flavor and color. Microwave drying works well for herbs such as parsley, chives and basil that loose much of their color drying more slowly.

For measurement purposes: one teaspoon of fresh herbs equals 1/4 teaspoon of dried herbs.

123

You'll have to experiment with the quantity and time it takes to dry since the water content in different leaves will evaporate in more or less time. To start, place a single layer of herbs on a microwave plate, cover with microwave paper and cook on high for about one minute. Check to see if the leaves are crisp. If not, microwave another thirty to sixty seconds. Be careful not to over-cook, as this will destroy the flavor. Keep a record of your time and results for future use. Store in the same manner as noted for hanging to dry.

Dehydrators can be used to dry herbs as well. Follow the instructions for your dehydrator.

Freezing Herbs

Herbs such as basil, chives, cilantro, dill and parsley retain so little of their flavor when dried that it's best to freeze them. Freezing retains color and flavor as well as most of the nutritive value of fresh young leaves. This has become the most popular way to preserve culinary herbs because it is convenient and fast.

The easiest way to freeze herbs is to simply pack them into plastic bags either singularly or in mixtures such as bouquet garni. Store the small packets in a larger rigid container in the freezer to avoid being damaged.

Small bunches of herbs like mints and chives can be wrapped in foil then stored in the freezer. The herbs can be cut off and chopped as needed.

Another simple method of freezing is to make herb ice cubes. Chop or puree the fresh leaves with a little water and put in ice cube trays. Once the herbs are frozen, store them in a labeled bag in the freezer. Add a cube to soups, stews or sauces as they cook; for measurement purposes, one cube equals one tablespoon.

Other Methods of Preserving Herbs

Herbs such as basil can be preserved in olive oil, layered with grated parmesan cheese, or layered with rock salt. French tarragon keeps well stored fresh in white wine vinegar.

ᴣ

As Erasmus said, "To have nothing here but sweet herbs, and those only choice ones too, and every kind its bed by itself."

124

August is the time to make your herb vinegars, oils, jellies and butters (see recipes beginning on page 177). All of these fun things make wonderful gifts for both fellow gardening friends and cooking enthusiasts.

Indoor Herb Gardening

Growing and using fresh culinary herbs all winter is a special treat. Now is not too early to start planning and preparing your winter windowsill herb garden. Indoor herb gardening is not diffi-cult. It only takes a little time and planning.

First determine what herbs you would like to grow and use. Here are some suggestions:

Bay laurel—tender perennial

Chervil—annual

Chives—perennial

Cilantro—annual

Curly or Italian parsley—biennial or annual

French tarragon—perennial

Greek oregano—perennial

Green sage—perennial

Lavender—tender perennial (flowers)

Lemon verbena—tender perennial

Mints—perennial

Nasturtiums—annual (flowers all winter)

Pineapple sage—tender perennial (flowers all winter)

Rosemary—tender perennial (flowers in January and February)

Scented geraniums—tender perennial

Sweet basil—annual

Sweet marjoram—annual

Thyme—perennial

Winter savory—perennial

August

It's best to start your plants in pots rather than digging them up from the garden; plants tend to go into shock when their roots are disturbed. There are several options for starting new plants. You can buy young transplants already started in pots; you can take cuttings from existing plants in your garden; or you can start from seed.

—— ❧ ——

Remember to transplant to larger pots as needed.

Before planting, sanitize your pots and trays in a mixture of one part bleach to nine parts water. Use clay or plastic pots with drainage holes if possible. Herbs like to be a little dry, so having drainage holes in the pots is important. Without drainage holes, the plants have a tendency to sit in too much moisture and rot.

A good soil is needed to get your plants off to a positive start. To keep pest problems on indoor plants to a minimum, a good rule of thumb is to use all bagged, sterilized soil. There are mixed potting soils available at garden centers or you can mix your own. Use a mixture of half bagged composted manure and half bagged soilless mix (peat moss, vermiculite and perlite, sometimes labeled germination mix). If the germination mix is not available, you can mix peat moss with bagged play sand. Whichever you choose, it is essential that the soil mix is well-drained.

From now until mid-September, keep your plants outside to encourage vigorous growth. As the weather begins to cool down, begin to move them indoors. It's good to get the plants adjusted to their new indoor growing environment before the heat in the house is turned on. Before bringing in, mix a solution of liquid dish detergent and water and mist the entire plant to prevent bringing in outdoor pests—especially aphids and whiteflies.

The best location for your indoor herb garden would be a place with southern exposure, a half day of sunlight and good ventilation. A secondary location would be a window facing east or west. The herbs' indoor home should be one with some fresh air but not a direct draft. The temperature should be between 50 and 70 degrees with an adequate amount of humidity. Most herbs dislike sudden changes in temperature, and they may not grow well in an area such as a small kitchen where there is heat fluctuation and cooking fumes.

Overwatering herbs is always a danger, so it's best to give your plants a good soaking once or twice a week. Use room temperature or tepid water, and occasionally mist the leaves with water. In order to create humidity for the plants, put some pebbles in the plant drainage trays.

Plants grown in pots soon use up the nutrients in the soil and should be fertilized each month with an organic fertilizer such as sea mix (fish emulsion and seaweed). This fertilizer has a sea smell so if your plants are in your kitchen, be sure to time your watering when the kitchen is not in use.

Keep in mind that while you will be able to enjoy the fragrance, color and flavor of your herbs throughout most of the winter, your plants will not grow as luxuriantly inside as outdoors. Basil, especially, becomes difficult to grow in the dead of winter as it prefers long sunny days and hot, humid weather, so don't be discouraged if it begins to look leggy.

All perennials will take a break and die back sometime around December and January for about six to eight weeks. Keep them cool and don't overwater. When you see signs of new growth, begin to increase watering and fertilizing.

Garden Notes:

Garden Notes:

───── ❧ ─────

Dill is a plant of good omen and in some European countries, the bride once put a sprig of dill and some salt in her shoes, as well as weaving a sprig on her dress.

─────────

SEPTEMBER

September To Do's

❧ Bring in tender perennials and windowsill plants to grow indoors. Be sure to spray before bringing in.

❧ Continue to harvest your herbs to be used in cooking and to make fresh wreaths and centerpieces.

❧ Mulch the garden to rebuild the soil.

❧ Begin a compost heap or add to one already going.

"My friend first points out on one side the beds of basil, burnet, chives, but as she turns to the other side her eyes sparkle with a happy light. For this is her tussie mussie garden, mignoneti, rosemary, lemon verbena…all of the old time favorites. Each plant is a personality, each kind of herb a fragrant memory for any visitor to the garden."

—Rosetta E. Clarkson

The Fall Garden

Autumn Moon

Autumn is not the only time of the year when the moon can be observed, but there are good reasons to associate it with this particular season. Cooling air and changing wind patterns have swept away the humid atmosphere of summer. The moon viewed on a cold October night is in sharp focus. It is possible to see craters and mountain ranges with only a pair of binoculars. Harvest moon, hunter's moon, the ghostly orb of Halloween—the moons of autumn are among the most memorable of the year.

The harvest moon is the full moon that occurs nearest the autumn equinox. It is so named for its tendency to continue rising early in the evening for several nights before and after full phase. For centuries farmers have taken advantage of the extra illumination and worked late to harvest their crops.

The autumn equinox officially begins September 22 or 23, when the noon sun is straight above the equator and day and night are affairs of equal duration everywhere on earth. By the calendar, it lasts until the winter solstice on December 21.

In October, a month after the autumn equinox, again there occurs extra illumination. This full moon is traditionally called the hunter's moon.

Indian Summer

As the weather continues to get colder in September and October, we are often relieved by a week or two of "Indian summer," that stretch of warm, hazy weather when the south winds blow up from the Gulf of Mexico to the central and eastern United States.

In the eighteenth century, western Pennsylvania was used as a reference point. It was here, during these warm weeks each year, that the term "Indian summer" came to be known. The Indians had a tradition of changing camps in the fall and moving to winter hunting grounds, sometimes attacking settlers as they relaxed during the warm weather.

Early settlers brought dill to North America, and this is where it became known as the "meeting seed" because children were given dill seed to chew during long church sermons.

Changes in the Garden

As September rolls around, there is a hint of autumn in the air; though the days may be warm and sunny, the evenings are cool. The herb garden in autumn has a special charm. The calm beauty of massed plantings of greens and grays is seen at its best.

The rows of basil are full and fragrant in the sun, with the green and purple leaves contrasting against the reds and yellows of the slowly ripening tomatoes! The summer savory with its reddish leaves covered with minute white blossoms and mints sprawling along pathways—all of these wonderful herbs waiting to be harvested.

The family of thymes are their greenest and grayest now, reaching safely under protective rocks for the winter. Many herbs have late blooms; mother of thyme often blooms for Thanksgiving. Pineapple sage, a tender perennial, begins blooming in October and, if brought indoors, will continue to send up its fragrant red spikes all winter long.

Using Herbs

The Europeans celebrate September 29, St. Michael's Day, as harvest time of fruits, vegetables, meats, grains, and honey—all of the foods that represent the bounty of nature and the richness of the harvest. It is during this season, this time of the year, that we are eager to use our fresh herbs in cooking and preserving. There is nothing that quite describes the flavor of freshly harvested herbs used in combination with other seasonal produce and meats.

This is the time of the year to make herb breads, herb butters and teas—all to be used now or frozen for use later. The air will be filled with good smells and when you open the kitchen door, the aroma of bread baking in the oven blends well with the bunches of mints and sage hanging to dry for winter teas (see page 189 for recipes).

Remember that basil is the first herb that will die once the weather dips below 50 degrees, so be sure to make your basil ice cubes and canned tomato sauce with fresh basil. Most importantly, take time to make basil pesto sauce to be used immediately, to be frozen or used in making pesto bread (see page 195 for recipe).

Bringing Plants Indoors

Indoor gardening can bring many hours of enjoyment. Whether you have room on your windowsill for plants or in front of a glass sliding door, bringing the plants indoors is a way of extending the growing season and enjoying the greenery.

Plants To Bring Indoors

Bring indoors those plants which are categorized as tender perennials such as bay laurel trees, lemon grass, lemon verbena, pineapple sage, rosemary and scented geraniums. These will not survive cold sub-zero winters.

Bay laurel, rosemary and scented geraniums continue to stay green all winter, thus providing wonderful color and aromas to fill the house!

If you have the light and space, try growing pineapple sage indoors. With long red spikes of three to four feet tall, pineapple sage begins to bloom in mid-October and continues until April or May. The pineapple scent and red flowers are an enjoyment hard to describe.

Hardy perennials, such as chives, Greek oregano, French tarragon, sage and thyme, can be brought indoors, but remember that even perennials will take a rest. For about two or three months they will die back.

In general, annuals like violets and nasturtiums that were growing in pots outdoors will have their lives extended only until November if brought indoors. It is a better idea to start with new, young annual plants that will give you blooms all winter.

How To Bring Plants Indoors

Plants in the ground may or may not make the transition of being dug up and put into a pot to be brought indoors. Once the roots are disturbed, the plants go into shock. The best way to move plants from the outdoors to the indoors is to plan ahead.

Plants that are in pots are easy to move indoors. In the spring, leave those plants that you plan to bring inside next winter in a pot and sink the pots in the ground. Then in the fall just dig up the pots and bring them in.

While the plants need to be brought indoors, we must be sure to leave the bugs and critters outdoors. Mix up a solution of one teaspoon liquid dish detergent to one quart of water and spray the plants you are bringing in. The soapy water clogs the pores of most bugs; they can not breathe and will die. Wash and sterilize the pots too, as bugs and eggs—even slugs—can easily attach themselves.

It's best to bring your plants indoors before you turn on the heat in the house. Make sure they are well watered, as the heat dries them out quickly.

Location of Indoor Plants

You will need to assess the best location for your plants. Most prefer at least a half day of good light, be it full sunlight or indirect light. The best is a southern exposure with direct sunshine and some shade. "Good indirect light" ideally means a northern exposure with plenty of sky light, though no direct sunlight will work, too.

Foliage plants prefer indirect light while most flowering plants need lots of sunshine. Flowering plants will continue to grow with less light but get long and spindly and will soon stop flowering.

Caring for Indoor Plants

After plants have been inside for awhile, check them regularly for bugs such as aphids, spider mites and whiteflies. The soapy water solution used when bringing the plants indoors should do the trick.

Keep the leaves free from dust by wiping with a damp cloth. A mixture of half water and half skimmed milk gives the leaves a good shine.

One factor to remember about bringing your plants inside for the winter months is that as the hours of daylight get shorter, the plants slow down their growth. Many will continue to stay green, but for the most part you will not see a surge of new growth in November, December or January. Of course there are exceptions—plants that bloom in the winter include African violets, amaryllis bulbs, Christmas cactus, pineapple sage and poinsettias.

Something you can do to trick hardy perennials into thinking that spring has arrived is to put the potted plants outdoors and let them freeze for about four to six weeks. It's good to do this in December, then plan to bring them back indoors about mid-January. They will start up again like spring. This will work for chives, garlic chives, French tarragon, lovage, mints, oregano, thyme and winter savory.

Rebuilding the Soil

Having a healthy garden depends on having good soil. The soil plays a major role in providing some of the things plants need: warmth, air, water and nutrients.

The structure of your soil, best described as the way in which the crumbs are arranged in groups, is far more important than the soil texture. These crumbs, or aggregates, are formed as decayed organic matter binds or glues soil particles together, giving the soil much more favorable qualities.

About 95 percent of soil consists of minerals, while only three to five percent of its total weight is organic matter. But one should never underestimate the importance of once-living material in the soil. It is something that must be renewed constantly if the soil is to stay in good condition. Organic matter is a major source of phosphorus and sulfur, the main source of energy for soil micro-organisms, and essentially the soil's only source of nitrogen.

Building up your soil means regular additions of organic matter in the form of manure, rotted leaves, compost, and the like. The use of organic amendments to your garden is really an investment in the future. After several years, the soil becomes darker in color, easier to work and faster to warm up in the spring. More earthworms should appear and hopefully your soil will need fewer waterings.

Building a garden soil is a long-term investment, but one that needn't involve any great cost. Keep a watchful eye for materials to add to the garden. Use green manure crops and cut the waste organic materials around your house and garden to a minimum.

Mulch

Mulch is a layer of material to be spread on the surface of the soil to retain moisture and retard weed growth. Mulch helps protect the soil from temperature extremes, keeping the ground warmer in winter and cooler in summer.

Organic mulches are good soil builders, although they will not increase fertility quickly. The benefits of mulch materials will be quickly realized when the materials are reduced in size by chopping or shredding to allow more exposure of the organic matter to decay organisms and water.

Most of the material used to make mulch are available free: leaves, leaf mold, pine needles, hulls or shells, corn cobs or stalks, woodchips or shavings, seaweed, sawdust, straw, spoiled hay, rotten wood and newspaper.

Ashes are a very good mulching material, and winter is a good time to collect wood ashes from your fireplace or woodburning stove. To get the most from your ashes, store them where the rain won't leach away the potash. A metal trash can works well. Ashes are very alkaline and have the same effect as spreading lime on the soil. Before planting in spring, work ashes into the top two to three inches of the soil.

Another item free and readily available every week is grass clippings. They are ideal for improving garden soil if handled properly. To use them as mulch material, you need to spread the grass very thinly when grass is green and dry. Take care not to spread many clippings in any one spot as grass will "burn" tender stems. Clippings can also be added to your compost pile, giving the nitrogen needed to make your pile "cook." Mix them well with other materials such as leaves, weeds or hay, spread them around the garden area then till them in. Grass also makes an excellent green manure (see page 143).

Mulch can be either worked into the soil or left on top of the soil each year. Leaving mulch in place on the surface replenishes the protective covering as it starts to decay on the soil surface. This is the closest imitation of natural fertilization that the home gardener can undertake. One single disadvantage is that mulched soils are very slow to warm up in the spring. The mulch can be pulled away, then put back in place when the crops begin to grow.

When mulch materials are returned to the soil, water and microbes begin the process of making the organic material available as plant food. Whether you till in your mulch or use it as a surface layer, it is one giant step toward rebuilding the soil and replenishing the nutrients for the next growing season.

Compost

There is a golden rule of gardening which states, "As long as there are wastes available, compost them!" When a product serves as many purposes in the garden as compost—fertilizer, soil amendment, weed suppressing mulch, pH adjuster, disease preventer, earthworm encourager, topsoil replenisher, erosion preventer—it pays to make it whenever you can, even now when the next gardening season seems so far away.

Home composting is duplicating what nature does all the time—recycling valuable nutrients. Naturally occurring soil organisms convert raw materials into dark-colored, nutrient-rich humus. Humus is more than just rotting organic matter. True humus has decomposed to the point where the original organic material can no longer be recognized. It is humus, in its gelatinous state, which surrounds soil particles and sticks them together into aggregates.

Compost provides a slow, steady supply of nutrients such as nitrogen, phosphorus and potassium as well as many of the essential micronutrients and elements. It allows a variety of nutrients to become available over a period of time that are not easily leached away.

Starting your own compost in the fall offers you a wide variety of ingredients that are available for the collecting. The greater the variety of organic matter, the better. The more diverse the mix, the more different types of micro-organisms will be at work.

Most gardeners feel that they can never get enough compost. You can keep your pile going year-round. Now that the leaves are falling from the trees and there are plenty of scraps from the garden and the kitchen, it is a perfect time to start your winter compost pile. There are two methods that can be used—piling compost or sheeting compost.

Compost Pile: A compost pile or heap should be built in layers consisting of two-thirds vegetative matter and one-third animal matter. The first layer could include items such as kitchen vegetable scraps, leftover garden greenery and alfalfa trimmings. Do not use any meats or fats from the kitchen as they do not break down. Fish and fish scraps, however, are ideal.

Layer number two could be straw, dried grass, leaves, cornstalks or woody plant stems. The third layer could be plain garden soil with all of its micro-organisms necessary for decomposing. The fourth layer could be animal manure from poultry, horse or cow. If seaweed or fish shells are available, they can also be added to this layer as they are great stimulators for a winter pile.

Remember to water down in between layers as the pile is being built, and turn it regularly. Continue to repeat the order of the layers. Your pile should be four to six feet high.

In order to keep your pile fairly active during the winter months, protect the decomposition process. Protection can be in the form of insulation to keep the pile warm. Bales of straw can be stacked around your compost pile. Straw allows air to enter and circulate, thus keeping the pile composting. Compost heaps enclosed by straw bales often do not need to be turned, they decompose all by themselves.

Sheet Composting: The second method is called sheet composting. In this method, you compost by spreading the raw ingredients directly on the soil surface then tilling them in. The layers of compost are not as deep as in the pile, so decomposition will occur more quickly.

The layers should include all of the same layers as pile composting. To heat up the mixture and speed up decomposition, spread three to six inches of leaves over the layers and sprinkle with ground limestone. Then till everything into the soil. The compost will start to break down, and when spring comes, till the soil again to complete the process. You will get the greatest improvement in the soil by tilling heavy applications of organic matter in the fall and letting it all compost right there over the winter.

Compost—nature's own soil improver. It's no wonder that most gardeners feel they can never get enough. Making compost not only enriches our lives but is good for the ecology and is in harmony with nature, recycling living matter.

Garden Notes:

OCTOBER

October To Do's

❧ Harvest the last of your herbs and prepare for Halloween with herbs to ward off witches.

❧ Prepare garden for winter by cutting perennials and mulching.

❧ Plant fall cover crops or "green manures" to add nutrients to the soil.

"Under the harvest moon,
when the soft silver
Drips shimmering
Over the garden nights,
Death, the gray mocker
Comes and whispers to you
As a beautiful friend
who remembers."

—Author unknown

As the days of brilliant sun grow shorter and moonlit nights get colder, the ghosts wander through the dying garden and lost spirits ride with the winds. The scent of autumn and the dying year is in the air, and it casts a curtain of magic over garden tasks. Cutting a long row of sage, picking pungent pennyroyal, gathering marigolds, bunching thyme for hanging, gathering tansy and bitter wormwood—regular autumn work just feels more magical at this time of year.

Halloween Lore

Harvesting the calendulas with their gold and orange disks, marigolds and bronzy chrysanthemums with their daisy-like odors, we are reminded that flowers with orange and yellow tones were considered protective plants against the evil charms of witchcraft. Their hot colors represent the fires which many careful witches would avoid.

Herbal folklore tells us that certain herbs would keep the witches away and guard us from harm during the Halloween season. There are nine such herbs you may want to grow and keep in the house to ward off the evil spirits and spells of the witches. The nine herbs are: betony, chamomile, fennel, plantain, nettle, thyme, watercress, wild apple and wormwood.

This herb charm dates back to the 1400s and was known to be chanted throughout the lands to ward off evil.

"Thyme and Fennel, two exceedingly might ones,

These herbs the wise Lord made.

Holy in the Heavens; He let them down,

Placed them and sent them into the seven worlds.

As a cure all, the poor and the rich,

It stands against pain, it dashes against venom,

Against the hand of an enemy and against the hand of the cursed,

And against the bewitching of many creatures."

—Author unknown

— ৯৯ —

Dill has long had a reputation for protecting against witchcraft and evil. It was also used by witches in spells and charms.

Autumn

We are now entering the resting season. The end of a cycle has come. The season of barrenness is upon us. Life in the garden has declined. And as the days shorten, we must remember that the warmth and light of summer brought us to the harvest of our garden's produce; now it's time to pass into autumn.

Autumn begins with a subtle change in the light, with skies a deep blue, and nights becoming suddenly clear and chilled. Most people who live in the northern states think of fall and winter in terms of frost and snow. Fall begins with the first frost, the disappearance of migrant birds, and the harvesting of the season's last crops. It ends with the first lasting snow.

In much of the world it is not autumn without autumn leaves. When the green forests grow spotted with yellow, orange and red, we know it is time to gather the crops, cut firewood and put up the storm windows.

Contrary to the old legend, Jack Frost does not paint the leaves with bright colors. The bright colors of autumn leaves and the subsequent dropping of those leaves are a precautionary tactic used by trees to protect themselves against the rigors of the winter season. As the cool weather approaches, trees cut back the flow of water to the leaves to conserve moisture and energy. This lack of water within the leaves causes them to change colors.

Mother Nature has given up her leaves for the gardener's benefit. Chop the leaves and use them as a mulch around the base of tender plants or as a blanket to cover the garden. The leaves will break down naturally, adding nutrients back to the soil. They can also be ground up and mixed in compost.

As the weather gets progressively colder in October, a week or two of Indian summer may occur. This stretch of warm, hazy weather is a time to clean the garden and ready it for a season of rest and regeneration.

Cleaning the Garden

As the evenings get cooler and plant growth slows down, the garden needs to be prepared for winter protection. One of the

problems in the first years of herb gardening comes in deciding what to cut back, what to leave, how much to mulch, what to bring indoors and what to leave out. These decisions must be made each autumn. Fortunately, most herbs are hardy perennials that need no winter coddling.

Cutting Back Herbs

Harvesting all summer and fall for seasonings and herbal arrangements will leave a minimal amount of material left in the garden. You may choose to cut the remaining branches and stems either in the fall, to make your garden look neat, or wait until next spring. Either way, trim branches back to an inch or two above the ground, gather up your clippings and add them to your compost pile.

Having the herb garden come through winter in good condition is of primary concern, so some may choose to let the frosted tops stand in the garden. There they catch the snow and hold it against the blustery winds, protecting the roots and crown from the harsh winter weather. Cutting can be done on the first days of spring when it's too early to remove mulches or to dig and plant. When spring comes to stay, gather clippings and add them to the compost pile.

Harvest your herbs, make up your herb vinegars and oils, dry them, preserve them for winter use, and cut stems and branches to make wonderful bouquets for drying.

Herbaceous perennials like artemesias, lemon balm, mints, rue, and tansy should be cut back to the ground. Lavender, santolina and germander are not cut back at all: My lavender bushes are never pruned except to remove blossoms, to make cutting for propagation or to clip for seasonings and wreaths. Cutting to the ground frequently kills lavender. These plants take three years to develop, so it is important to preserve the wood from season to season. There are bound to be some winter casualties, so take some cuttings from your tender perennials now. The herbs from which cutting may be taken include bay laurel, lemon verbena, myrtle and rosemary, as well as other shrubby herbs. (See page 63 for information on taking cuttings.)

The tender perennial plants that were put outside in pots in May and sunk into the garden can now be dug out. Trim back about one-third of the top growth. These potted plants should gradually be introduced into the house before the heat is turned on.

Mulching

Fall is the time to mulch the entire garden, some plants more heavily than others. You can use grass clippings, leaves, compost or salt hay. Do not mulch until the top two inches of soil is frozen. If a deep mulch is placed down before the topsoil freezes, field mice and rodents may find a warm refuge and cause damage. However, if you wait to mulch until after some sharp freezes, the soil will have been put to sleep by the anesthetic of autumn's decreasingly warm days and increasingly cold nights.

Old-time gardeners made mulch in the form of leaf mold. They would dig a hole in the corner of their garden and, using beech, oak or elm leaves, alternate layers of leaves with horticultural lime to decay over the winter. Despite their great value in the garden, decaying leaves also become a great place for insects to lay eggs. Before using the leaf mold, gardeners would mix it with soot or horticultural lime which would destroy most infestations. A mixture of one-half cup ammonia per gallon of water sprinkled over the leaf mold heap will also help to kill the insects. However, it is best to use leaf mold on outdoor plants only and not on potted plants that come indoors.

Green Manure

If your soil has been neglected for many years, it will most likely take more than a year to restore it to a productive, fertile state. Nature does things gradually, but there are some things that the gardener can do to create ideal conditions and give nature a boost.

October

A cover crop, or green manure, may be just the boost your garden needs. Green manures are crops grown simply for the purpose of being chopped and mixed directly back into the soil. Growing green manures is an outstanding technique for improving soil texture, increasing its humus content, and building up the available supply of topsoil plant nutrients. Plants grow by drawing nutrients from the soil. When they die, they return to the earth those nutrients that were used in growing.

Benefits of Green Manure

1. With green manures, you can avoid the time and work of collecting and hauling organic matter to your garden.

2. Green manure is a very economical source of organic matter.

3. Once a green manure crop has been turned under, it provides excellent food for earthworms; the worms ingest and digest organic matter, producing fertile granular castings which are rich in plant nutrients. The presence of earthworms in the soil is evidence of good microbial activity.

4. The roots of many green manure crops reach deep into the subsoil, absorbing valuable nutrients and bringing them up into the plant tissues. When the crop is turned under, these nutrients will revitalize the topsoil.

5. Certain crops called legumes can capture and fix large amounts of nitrogen from the air. Legumes add more of this important plant nutrient to the soil when tilled under than they consumed while growing. Nitrogen is essential for plant growth.

6. Depending upon your specific soil profile, growing green manures can cut down on your need to purchase fertilizers and other soil additives and conditioners. An effective green manuring program can reduce by about one-half the fertilizer needs of the average garden.

7. A green manure garden becomes more and more weed-free every year because the crops choke out weeds.

8. The organic matter from green manures—particularly the legumes—is more rapidly available to the plants than that from many other types of soil amendments. Turned under when the growth is succulent and well filled with water, the plants decompose rapidly. The nitrogen added by leguminous varieties hastens this process even further. The rapid breakdown of the organic matter means that succeeding crops will benefit quickly from the plant foods being thus liberated.

In the language of flowers and herbs, chives have come to be known as the devil's right footprint.

To grow green manures, it is ideal to have two plots. While one is in use for vegetable production, the other can be used for the growth of soil-improving cover crops. Alternating the cropping pattern allows for steady improvement in both areas.

If you have space enough to expand your current garden, consider this alternating approach. Even if you can't double your current space, creating room enough for the growth of cover crops every year over a third of the space would prove of definite benefit.

Ryegrass

One of the green manures to be considered for fall planting is ryegrass, an annual. Within a few weeks of planting, a green manure crop of ryegrass will form a light green blanket of grass and roots; this will benefit your garden even if it only grows a few inches before winter sets in. The tight web of roots will hold the soil securely and stop erosion that could result from wind and rain. It will also prevent needless evaporation of moisture from uncovered soil.

The next spring, a thick matting of dead ryegrass will be appear under the snow. Already the dead and decomposing grass and roots are providing food for the earthworms. Once the soil has warmed up sufficiently, the ryegrass can be chopped up and spaded or tilled under. After tilling any kind of organic material it is best to wait ten days to two weeks before planting.

If a perennial crop that survives the winter, such as a rye, is grown, it should be allowed to grow up again in the spring before tilling it under. This gives a double helping of organic matter. Because of the waiting period before planting, the area in which a perennial green manure was grown will have to be reserved for a late-planted crop.

Buckwheat

It's hard to beat buckwheat as a green manure for impoverished soil. It will grow in sand, clay and overly dry or wet areas. It may look scraggly and reflect the poor soil quality, but at least it provides a cover crop.

Like rye, buckwheat produces a lot of organic material very quickly. It's especially good for loosening up tough sod and killing weeds and lawn grasses when you're making a brand-new garden.

Buckwheat, which can be broadcast by hand, is much hardier than most of the other grains, such as wheat, corn and oats. It does particularly well in the northern regions of the Midwest. Buckwheat is actually a summer green manure. It's best to sow it when the ground is thoroughly warmed in summertime, during June or July, after you've harvested your peas and other early crops. It will reach the blossom stage in six or eight weeks. Before buckwheat blossoms, it can be harvested as a mulch. After it blossoms it can be used as chicken feed; when seeds are fully mature, they can be used for making buckwheat flour.

Honeybees swarm to buckwheat blossoms as pollen is often hard to find at that time of year. Buckwheat honey is rich, dark and flavorful.

In late summer, a rear-end rotary tiller can be used to chop up and turn under a hip-high growth of buckwheat. A better alternative to turning under your buckwheat crop is to mow it down and leave it. The seeds will settle in the loosened soil and replant the crop the following spring. This way you can get two green manure crops from a single sowing if your soil really needs improvement and if you can wait that long before planting a food crop. To get rid of buckwheat permanently, be sure to till it under after it blossoms but before the seeds develop.

Legumes

Legumes have a very special importance when used for soil improvement. They attract certain types of soil microbes to their roots; these microbes extract nitrogen from the air and convert it into a form usable by the plants. Therefore, a legume actually returns more nitrogen to the soil than it used in growing.

To make sure that nitrogen-fixing microbes are present, it's usually recommended that you inoculate legume seeds with a mixture of these tiny creatures before planting. The inoculant culture, which comes as a dark powder, can be purchased from most suppliers of legume seeds. Mix the inoculant with water according to the directions and evenly coat the seeds.

For those of us who live close to nature, with our working days spent growing, cultivating, harvesting and using herbs from the garden and the field, it is fun to spend the evenings discovering the intriguing plant histories that add fascination to our gardening life. "Sleeping With a Sunflower" by Louise Riotte and many of Adelma Simmons' books make delightful reading.

Clover: Clover is the best-known legume. There are many kinds of perennial clovers. Vetch and clover crops should be allowed to grow at least one full season, perhaps two, to get the maximum benefit from nitrogen fixation and green growth. A disadvantage to leaving them for several years is that they sometimes become difficult to destroy completely. Alsike clover has the benefit of growing on ground too wet for the red clovers. Honeybees love clover blossoms.

Vetch: Hairy vetch, one of the many types of vetch, is a perennial but is relatively slow-growing. It's good to plant a fast-growing annual "nurse crop" like rye or oats along with the inoculated vetch seed to provide shade and check competitive weed growth. Rye also gives support to the vine-like growth of vetch.

Soybeans: Another good edible legume is the common soybean, which is becoming increasingly important as a true meat substitute. Soybeans are the only vegetable that has the essential proteins of meat. A crop of soybeans can, of course, be grown strictly as a green manure. They will greatly improve the soil in just one season.

Alfalfa: From all the research that's been done, it seems that alfalfa is number one when it comes to green manures. American farmers and gardeners realize the value of this legume. It is estimated that over one-third of all the hay produced in our country is now alfalfa. It's one of the most palatable and nutritious foods for livestock, so it must be a delicacy for earthworms, too.

Alfalfa is right on top in terms of protein content, which breaks down into usable nitrate "fertilizer." Alfalfa's nitrogen content is considerably higher than that of most legumes. Its leaves and stalks store up many more nutrients than they use in growing. Alfalfa also contains calcium, magnesium, manganese, phosphorus, potassium and zinc, which makes it a nearly complete natural fertilizer.

Some green manure crops, such as alfalfa, will give the greatest benefit if left growing for more than one year. Others are short-season crops that can be returned to the soil in six weeks.

Weeds

Are weeds a green manure crop? Yes. These guardians of the soil must not be overlooked. They are Mother Nature's most common green manure. Weeds help to correct for nutrient and trace-mineral imbalances in a soil. Most weeds are very deep-rooted and draw valuable elements up to the topsoil. We think of them as a nuisance because they compete with other crops, but in that idle section of your garden, they're busy at work, if only keeping the topsoil covered and intact. Just be sure to till them under before they go to seed, especially if you intend to plant food crops in that spot next year.

Except for legumes, which contain their own supply of nitrogen, the decomposition of green manure crops can be hastened by spreading a high nitrogen fertilizer, such as blood meal, about two weeks before the crop is to be turned under.

Turn under a green manure crop when it is actively growing, tender and succulent. When the water supply is within the plant, the process of decay will proceed much faster than if the dead organic matter must draw its water from the soil.

Decomposition of the organic matter will be greatly retarded if the plants are allowed to reach a woody state. And never allow the green manure crop to go to seed. A weed has been defined as a plant out of place, and it holds true for alfalfa as well as for crabgrass.

Once you see the improvement that comes from green manuring, you'll try not to let bare parts of your garden waste valuable growing time again.

Garden Notes:

Tarragon was once the ingredient in love potions.

NOVEMBER

November To Do's

৵ Enjoy herbal scents in your home—make fireplace bundles, laundry rinse, sachets and hot pads.

৵ Brew herbal teas using dry, fresh, or frozen herbs.

৵ Harvest the last of your sage and use it in holiday cooking.

৵ Winter mulch after hard frost.

৵ Do not fertilize your indoor potted herbs in November, December or January, as these are slow growing months and there is little plant growth. This is a good time to repot your plants— before the spring growth begins.

"The fogs and excess of atmospheric humidity render this the most cheerless month of the year and therefore every effort should be made to maintain the conservatory and other structures devoted to ornamental plants."

—"The Garden Oracle," 1896, about the month of November

Using Herbs in the Home

What better way to turn a cheerless month into a cheerful month than to begin to fill the house with the scents of the upcoming holiday season.

Since the earliest of times, people have taken herbs from the garden, fields and forests to scent their homes. Egyptians put flowers and spices in their tombs, Romans perfumed their linens with lavender and stuffed their mattresses with dried rose petals.

In medieval times, royal households as well as those of simple peasants, tossed pungent herbs such as rosemary and thyme on the floor where they released their fresh scent when walked upon. Gardens of sweet-smelling herbs such as roses and lavender were the source of potpourri to scent the house.

In these fast paced times, there has been a rediscovery of that pleasure that comes from filling our homes with fragrance. Potpourris, pomander balls, scented candles and pine cones, fireplace bundles, mini spice wreaths and fresh holiday greens will fill your house with smells that will last throughout the season.

All of these scents make great family projects on cold, dreary days. (See page 209 for more uses and gift ideas.)

The Greeks believed that thyme invigorated its warriors. Romans bathed in thyme water for increasing energy.

Fireplace Bundles

One way for you to continue to enjoy all of the wonderful smells of summer is by making fireplace bundles. As you harvest and dry herbs such as thyme, rosemary, oregano, mints, lavender and any others that you will be cutting back, collect the woody stems. Once dried, you can put them together into six- to eight-inch bundles of branches, add in some of your dried flowers for color and tie them with colorful raffia. As the days and nights get cooler and you begin using your fireplace, toss in one of your bundles to release its pleasant scent.

Laundry Fresheners, Sachets and Hot Pads

There are many ways to use the flowers and herbs that we collected and dried all season long. Lavender, for instance, can make a fragrant floral rinse water to scent the laundry or lavender buds can be placed in a small cotton bag and tossed in the dryer, giving the laundry a fresh clean smell. Bunches of lavender can be hung in closets to add fragrance, too.

Little sachets of moth-repellent herbs such as southernwood, tansy or santolina can be tucked among precious woolens. Sachets filled with many mixtures of dried flowers and herbs can be hung in closets, on the arms of chairs and even on door knobs. Or you can make sweet pillows and tuck them behind cushions where they will release their fragrance when leaned upon.

Tea time is even more enjoyable when the tea cozy is stuffed with herbs and spices that release their pungent aromas when placed over the hot tea pot. On this idea, hot pads filled with fragrant mixtures will give your kitchen all of those great aromas.

Because hot pads are used with food, it's best to fill them with herbs used in the kitchen such as lemon balm, lemon verbena, rosemary, thyme and rich spices. These are to be used as a trivet for hot pots or tea kettles where the heat of the pot will release the wonderful aromas of the herbs.

Make a double thickness square or any other shaped pouch. Sew up three sides, fill it with your mixture then sew up the fourth side.

A simple mixture would be:

> 1   *cup rosemary*
>
> 1/2   *cup thyme*
>
> 1/2   *cup lemon balm or verbena*
>
> 1   *tablespoon small cinnamon chips*
>
> 1   *teaspoon ground cloves (whole cloves can be used, too)*

Herbal Teas

As we move into the winter months and begin to spend more time indoors, it's a wonderful opportunity to brew up some herbal teas from your garden. Hot herbal teas give a great deal of enjoyment on a cold, snowy day. Sitting by the fire and sipping the hot fragrant tea slowly, thinking of gardens, music, books, poems and quiet things, is a great prescription for a winter afternoon.

——— 🍂 ———

*"Winter seems to me
A time for tea
when all the garden
Is at rest
To sit and sip
Is best."*

—*Adelma Grenie
Simmons*

Most herbal teas are great to enjoy mid-afternoon for a pick-me-up. Make tea-time a social gathering of gardening friends by asking each to bring herbs or flowers to add to the brew. And, of course, hot herbal tea can be served with herbal cookies and tea cakes for a complete mid-day break.

If you've been fortunate to be able to bring your herb plants and scented geraniums indoors, you've got your supply. If you don't have the room or light to grow herbs indoors, don't fret; you too can enjoy herbal teas. Certainly if you planned ahead and dried leaves to use during winter cooking, you've prepared. (See page 189 for herbal tea recipes.)

Sage

Sage was honored by the Chinese as a symbol of immortality; they traded three pounds of the choicest tea for one pound of sage. John Gerard in his 1633 herbal maintained that "it is singularly good for the head and brain, it quickeneth the sense of memory, strengthen the sinews, restoreth health to those that have palsy and taketh away shakey trembling of the members."

And no turkey worth its salt (or lack of salt) is complete without sage. Back many years ago when the first Thanksgiving was celebrated, they found and used sage in preparation for the festive dinner. Thanksgiving has always been associated with a bountiful harvest—a feast shared with family and friends, and sage is a perfect complement to the flavors of the feast. Plan to use the sage from your garden this holiday season. Sage leaves can be put under the skin of poultry for a greater flavor from the meat itself.

Common garden sage is the cornerstone of the herb garden. It is a hardy perennial that holds its own even after a heavy frost. Its gray foliage braves the cold and even as the winter snow appears, it usually hangs on until the end of November before taking its winter's rest. This is the time to have your final harvesting of sage.

Fresh sage has a prominent lemon zest flavor that is lessened when the herb is dried. Fresh sage can be frozen by placing whole sprigs in plastic zipper storage bags and freezing.

If you plan to dry sage for winter use, it needs to be done carefully as the heavy leaves and thick stems can retain moisture,

"Sage maketh the lamp of life, so long as nature lets it burn, burn brightly."

—Author unknown

creating a musty taste when stored in a covered container. As with most herbs, store in the largest bits possible. It is best not to grind the leaves for storing as it destroys the lemony taste, leaving only the harsher camphor flavor.

As you enjoy your Thanksgiving meal, think of this ancient proverb from the Orient, "How can a man grow old who has sage in his garden?"

Winter Mulching

In early November we should wrap up the last of the gardening chores. One of these chores is mulching. While in the summer we mulch to keep the soil cooler and help it to retain moisture and cut down on weeds, at this time of the year we are mulching to help protect the soil from temperature extremes, keeping the ground warmer in the winter. Unprotected plants are subject to alternating thawing and freezing, a situation that damages the root systems. Mulching in winter protects perennials from this stress.

Mulch materials that can be used are leaves, leaf mold, pine needles, seaweed, wood chips and shavings, spoiled hay, straw, rotted wood, hulls and shells, corn cobs or stalks, newspaper and any other scrap material that will decompose. Leaves usually take two years to decompose in your compost pile so it is best to shred them up before using so that they will also allow air to circulate.

Using salt hay or hay without weed seeds as the first layer will also allow air to circulate. Be cautious not to use heavy layers of grass clippings as they tend to clump into a soggy mess when they get wet. Saw dust can also be used since it is light, airy and free of weed seeds. It not only holds in the moisture, but as it decomposes, it helps to improve the soil. Wood ashes from the fireplace will add valuable potash to your soil; use sparingly due to its high alkaline content.

As a rule of thumb, wait until the ground freezes before putting a heavier mulch down; otherwise small animals will make a home in it, using your plant's roots for food. Once the ground freezes you will also avoid the risk of mildew. When cold weather sets in, fungus won't flourish—it goes dormant. Indian summer keeps these plants alive and when the plants have not become dormant, they are still vulnerable to mildew-prone conditions encouraged by premature winter mulching.

Most gardeners prefer to turn the winter's mulch directly into the soil in the spring. Then the action of water and microbes can start the process of making organic material available as plant food. Others leave the mulch in place year after year, replenishing the protective covering as it starts to decay on the soil surface. This is the closest imitation of natural fertilization that the home gardener can undertake, and after a period of a few years, it will yield noticeable benefits.

A single disadvantage is that mulched soils are very slow to warm up in the spring. The mulch can be pulled away, then put back in place when the plants begin to grow. Soil erosion from wind and water is minimized in a mulched garden.

A blanket of snow makes a wonderful insulator. Snow was once regarded as a "poor man's fertilizer" for its insulating qualities and for the modest amount of atmospheric nitrogen it washes down into the soil.

Waiting to Clean the Garden

If you don't have time to cut back the old foliage, the plants will flop over by themselves or you can smash them down over the crown of the plant, where the top of the plant and the root base meet, where new growth will sprout. The old foliage mulch actually shades the plant from the sun, keeping it from freezing and thawing. This alternating of cold and warm temperatures is hard on plants. The old foliage will also catch the snow and hold it in place.

And if you're one of those who puts off cleaning the garden beds until the end of the season, don't feel guilty. If for some reason the garden doesn't get cleaned up until next spring, the plants will survive. One factor that is of importance is that garden pests set up household in dead foliage left about the garden over the winter. It's best to move it to the compost pile to decompose, unless you want to start out spring with your garden pests already in place.

Garden Notes:

DECEMBER

December To Do's

❧ Enjoy the tastes and smells of your preserved herbs.

❧ Decorate your home with the herbs of Christmas and share their stories with others.

"Silly gardener! Summer goes
And winter comes with pinching toes,
When in the garden bare and brown
You must lay your barrow down!"

—R.L. Stevenson

The Winter Solstice

The month of December ushers in many European festivals and celebrations leading up to the largest one—Christmas itself. From the old herbals, calendars, prints and books come the customs and celebrations that revolve around nature, the garden and, of course, the coming of winter solstice.

The days leading up to the winter solstice, on December 22, are the darkest days of the year. Life for that time seems dormant when the sun is at its farthest point from the earth.

St. Thomas' Day, December 21, the shortest day of the year and the longest night, is said to be the turning point of the gardener's year. This festival has been celebrated for centuries, with the festivities linked to the fertility of the soil and the longed-for return of the sun.

"Onion skins
very thin,
Mild winter
coming in.
Onions skins
thick and tough,
Coming winter
very rough."

—Cotswold saying

Many traditions grew up regarding the planting of seeds at this time of the year. In the southeast of England, broad beans would be planted on this day and the wise gardener would check the skin of his onions on St. Thomas' Day to ascertain the weather for the coming winter months.

December 14 to 28, the seven days before and after St. Thomas' Day, were known as Halcyon Days. The old name for the kingfisher was halcyon, and it was thought that at this time the gods granted a respite from winter storms to this lovely bird to enable her to hatch her young in peace.

Christmas Eve, December 24, is the day to take precautions to ensure a good crop of fruit. On Christmas Eve, straw should be bound around the trunks of all fruit trees. Fruit props cut on this day, when the sap is low, will last forever, so it is said.

As the earth lies dead and cold, the rich scents of the holiday herbs remind us of growing things, of sunshine and gentle rains. The evergreens, fragrant and bright, speak of life everlasting.

The lore that surrounds mid-winter greenery reaches back through the dark corridors of uncertain times when, as days shortened, our ancestors were terrified lest they would be overwhelmed by cold and darkness. As the days raced toward the winter solstice, the day of the longest night, fires were lit and living greens were gathered in tribute to those spirits who controlled the seasons. It is with this long night, a time of rest in the garden, that our year truly begins.

We are all but a tiny part of the ever-moving stream of the seasons and the years that slip by without our notice. Sit back and think of the generations who have greeted the winter solstice with the same scent filling their nostrils. It is a time for reflection, a time to celebrate.

Enjoying Herbs in Winter

There is a feeling that we need to bring light and warmth to this cold period, and it is a time in which we begin to light the fire in the fireplace.

As dusk falls, we touch a flame to kindling and candles, and by fire and candlelight enjoy the pungent fragrance of fresh evergreens and rosemary, and the sweet spice of newly made pomanders. Piled by the hearth are fireplace bundles made from herbs no longer useful for cooking, and we burn these fragrant offerings that remind us of our summer gardens.

When all is cold and dreary outside, it is the time to take the lids off bottles and inhale the scents of summer: to smell the concentrated fragrance of dried herbs; to stir potpourri and feel the fragile smoothness of paper-thin rose petals and the brittle fabric of pungent geranium leaves, while the soft aroma drifts upward; to see that clove pomanders are hanging in closets to keep clothes fresh and free from hibernating insects; and to unfold chilly sheets, smelling sweet and sunny of verbena and lavender that have been dried in the linen cupboard.

Among the herbs of particular interest now are hyssop, marjoram, oregano, rosemary, sage, savory and thyme. These plants possess vital life-giving forces in their every part: root, stalk, leaves and flowers are permeated with a cheery vigor that helps drive away chills while warming and harmonizing the system—qualities especially welcome during cold weather.

Although these sturdy perennials grow throughout summer and have many uses in hot weather cooking, one of their particular virtues is their ability, fresh or dried, to enliven heavier foods.

Their aromatic spiciness combines well with robust dishes, and their nutritional contribution is high. Plan to use your herbs in seasonal specialties.

The Traditional Herbs of Christmas

Fir trees and pine boughs, holly and balsam are all well-loved and long-used Christmas greens. However, there are other greens—herbal greens—that also have a strong association with the holidays.

——— ॐ ———

*"Hemlock and cedar,
Rosemary, thyme
and basil,
Frankincense and
myrrh,
Mistletoe, fir
and the sweet
spice of the east."*

—*William
Hamilton*

Rosemary, thyme, lavender and rue; pennyroyal, bedstraw, horehound, sweet woodruff, chamomile and the little star-of-Bethlehem are all related to the Christmas story. As a group, they are traditionally called cradle or manger herbs, though not all are said to have been used in the manger.

The stories that go with the manger herbs are as old and as charming as Christmas itself. On winter nights proceeding the excitement of Christmas Eve, it's fun to sit in front of a blazing fire and retell the old, not-so-familiar stories to the children. Bits of each plant can be passed around for tasting and smelling for complete enjoyment.

Rosemary

The symbol of remembrance, rosemary is the chief herb of Christmas. This native plant of the Mediterranean has one legend which tells how the plant acquired its beautiful flowers.

All rosemary, according to legend, bore pure white flowers until the shrub offered shelter to the Holy Family during their flight into Egypt. Exhausted and dirty, the family took refuge in a thick stand of rosemary on the bank of a brook to spend a day and night resting and laundering.

Mary, after a good sleep, washed the baby's swaddling clothes and her own cloak in the brook. She spread the wash on the thick, soft, fragrant branches of the flowering rosemary to dry. When the garments were removed, the white flowers had changed to the soft blue of Mary's mantle. The swaddling clothes retained the clean, refreshing scent of rosemary.

This legend prompted mothers in the Middle Ages to slip a sprig of rosemary into their baby's cradle so the child might have a sweet and peaceful sleep. To this day, rosemary usually bears blue flowers, though an occasional white or pink can still be found.

Rosemary is said to bring happiness to families who use it to perfume the house on Christmas night. Some believe rosemary blooms on January 6, the Epiphany, or the Twelfth Day of Old Christmas. A popular medieval New Year's gift was a sprig of rosemary and an orange stuck with cloves (today we know this as a pomander ball).

Use rosemary, in combination with rosehip berries, in your holiday wreaths and centerpieces for a rich fragrance throughout the house. Fresh rosemary sprigs can be used and allowed to dry in place. Sprigs dried in the summer can be combined with the fresh at Christmastime. You can never have too much rosemary.

Rosemary plants are unsurpassed as gifts or tokens of appreciation. Because the plants are easy to grow, the sentiment remains a permanent expression.

Rosemary has been carried at weddings to represent the fidelity of lovers and gilded sprigs were exchanged as tokens between friends.

Our Lady's Bedstraw or Cradlewort

Legend holds that the fragrant golden flowers of Our Lady's bedstraw or cradlewort, were once white and scentless, but on the first Christmas Eve when it became apparent that the Christ child was about to be born, Joseph quickly cleaned the old hay from the manger and replaced it with freshly cut armfuls of bedstraw and other grasses. After the baby was wrapped in clean clothes, he was gently laid in the freshly filled manger. The white flowers of the bedstraw turned a shining gold and a wonderful fragrance filled the air.

To this day, this species of bedstraw has golden puffs of scented flowers. Bedstraw is a hardy perennial that blossoms in late June and can be hung to air dry to use at Christmas. They can make satisfying houseplants, too.

December

Rue

Shakespeare's "herb of grace," rue symbolizes vision, virginity and repentance. It is frequently associated with St. Lucy, Virgin

Martyr and protector of eyesight, whose feast day, December 13, marks the beginning of the Christmas season in Sweden.

Rue is a shrubby, sea green perennial that produces small yellow flowers all summer. It stays green well into winter and has attractive bead-like seed pods that can be used for decoration along with its leaves.

Pennyroyal

Pennyroyal is said to bloom on Christmas Day, at least in Sicily. An old herbal has recorded that "the children of Sicily always put pennyroyal amongst the green things in their creches and believe that exactly at midnight it bursts into flower for Christmas Day."

The Christmas pennyroyal is a tiny, creeping mint, sometimes called English pennyroyal. It is not as winter hardy as other types of mints and needs the protection of mulching. It can be used in holiday bouquets and nosegays. It has the tendency to become brittle when dried, so misting and gentle handling are advised.

Horehound

Horehound is one of the five bitter herbs of Passover. Tradition says it was mixed with sweet grasses in the manger. It is used at Christmas as a symbol of the Holy Family's flight to Egypt and is considered to be a manger herb. It is a hardy perennial that can be cut during the growing season and dried for use at Christmas.

Chamomile

Chamomile symbolizes patience and energy-in-adversity. The plant is native to Palestine and some stories say that it was among the herbs in the manger hay. To this day, it blooms during hay season in that part of the world.

The early Christian church dedicated the humble apple-scented chamomile to St. Anne, mother of the Virgin Mary. This plant is a perennial which produces tiny daisy-like flowers that

160

can be hung to dry. They will retain their color, shape and scent for many months.

Star-Of-Bethlehem

The modest little spring flower star-of-Bethlehem is another herb closely bound to Christmas tradition. The story is told that after the bright guiding star had led the wise men to the stable, it exploded. As the tiny pieces of the expended star fell to the earth, they turned into small, white star-shaped flowers, named star-of-Bethlehem.

Another story places the plant in the manger where the Babe was laid to sleep. It suddenly bloomed in the form of a wreath around his head. This legend contends that the Christ child himself named the flower star-of-Bethlehem.

These flowers come from bulbs which multiply and spread. The flowers and leaves can be picked in spring and dried or pressed for Christmas use.

Lavender

Lavender symbolizes purity. It is said to derive its refreshing, clean scent from the Holy Infant's clothes. A medieval legend says that lavender was scentless until Mary laundered the garments of the Baby and spread them upon a lavender bush. After they had dried and whitened in the sun, she folded the clothes and took them home. Never again was lavender scentless.

Lavender is a perennial that will thrive happily if given three things—sweet soil, excellent drainage and protection against frost-heaves during winter thaws. It flowers in the summer and can be dried for use as it retains its scent and color for years.

Wild Thyme

Legend holds that bits of wild thyme, symbol of strength and activity, and sweet woodruff, symbol of humility, were found among the dried grasses that formed the birth bed of the Virgin Mary. Wild thyme is a cousin to the English-French culinary thyme and is especially happy growing around rocks as it is a creeping variety. It can be cut during the growing season, dried and used for winter decorating.

Sweet Woodruff

Sweet woodruff is the herb of May. It is a low-growing, shade-loving perennial ground cover. Fresh woodruff has no appreciable scent, but as the plant dries, it develops a bewitching vanilla-hay odor. The scent of dried sweet woodruff was dearly loved in the Middle Ages.

May the symbolism and cultivation of the Christmas herbs brighten your holidays.

"For somehow, not only at Christmas, but
all the long year through, the joy that
you give to others is the joy that
comes back to you."

—John Greenleaf Whittier

Garden Notes:

CONTAINER GARDENING

Container gardening is more popular today than ever, and for a good reason. It is a boon for people who live in an apartment, a condo and even a home where they may be blessed with ample garden space but do not want to be bending and digging in the soil.

Whether you have a tiny backyard, a patio or deck, with imaginative containers, a good soil mix, adequate moisture, a supply of nutrients and good basic gardening practices you will have a container garden to be enjoyed all summer long.

Containers

There are a wide variety of containers for you to choose from for your outdoor garden. The different sizes, shapes and colors of your containers can combine to make attractive groupings on a patio or terrace. Or perhaps you'd prefer a variety of herbs in a single display, planted in a barrel cut in half or a wood planting tub.

The traditional terra-cotta flower pot has been used in gardens since Roman times. Until recently this type of pot was only made out of terra-cotta, a once-fired porous red clay, which is very attractive. This highly porous material absorbs a lot of moisture from the potting mixture. This moisture then evaporates into the air. Before planting in terra-cotta pots, soak the pots thoroughly in ensure the new plant will have plenty of water. All plants in terra-cotta pots require more frequent watering than plants in plastic pots.

Terra-cotta can crack and flake with weathering in very cold temperatures. Sometimes elements are added to the clay before it is fired to make it frost-proof. Because of the cold conditions in the Midwest, make sure that the terra-cotta you buy has been

> *In Italy, a pot of basil placed on a balcony means a woman is ready for a suitor to arrive, and if he brings her a sprig of basil, she would surely fall in love with him.*

treated this way. Now available, too, are a wide variety of decorative, glazed ceramic pots from Europe. They also tend to be less frost-proof and the glaze will crack, so be sure to look for the frost-resistant pots for your plants.

You can also make a simple container by slitting plastic bags of soil mix and setting transplants directly into the bag. Or consider recycling baby bathtubs, leaky buckets, plastic milk jugs, and any other containers that otherwise may clog a landfill.

Tall pots and barrels with numerous openings up the sides allow many plants to grow in a small space, which justifies the extra care and attention that they need. Whether you plant your herbs in a traditional earthenware strawberry pot or design one of your own, be sure to turn the pot each week, so that each side gets an equal amount of sunshine during the growing season. Do this just before watering, when the pot is the lightest.

Herbs, such as parsley and thyme, are suited for hanging baskets, where they may be interplanted with flowering annuals. The soil in these plant containers tends to dry out rapidly so not all plants can be grown in them. Wire baskets should be lined with dampened living sphagnum moss, green side outward—the larger the pieces of moss, the longer it will live. Fill up the basket with a light soil mixture, the same as you would use for potted plants, and plant the basket with smaller plants to allow for growing room. Keep well watered and fertilized.

When choosing a container, be sure to pick one that will be large enough to handle the mature plant. Two-gallon tubs or baskets are large enough to support vigorously growing perennial herbs such as mint and rosemary. Eight- to 12-inch pots are sufficient for basil and lavender. And even four- to six-inch pots will support chives, dill, parsley and thyme. A box planter under a kitchen window is a convenient place to grow chives, parsley and other low-growing herbs so you can snip quickly while cooking.

Whatever container you choose, there needs to be holes at the bottom so that excess water drains away. Otherwise your plants can easily become waterlogged and drown. Drainage holes are also important for flushing water through the soil to dissolve accumulated salts.

Plants

When mixing herbs together in one container, be sure to combine compatible plants with similar needs and growing conditions. Shrubby herbs, such as thyme, which love good drainage and enjoy sunlight, will not be too happy combined with a water-loving mint. For the most part, herbs are quite easy to cultivate and will survive together because they are basically hardy and good-natured plants.

A container can also be a good way to keep invasive herbs in check. Mints, for example, are rapid spreaders and could take over wherever they are planted. But grown in a container, their roots are safe from causing harm to other smaller plants.

Soil

The soil mix for plants in containers should be light, airy and capable of holding moisture and nutrients, yet quick to drain. A common mixture would be one part potting soil, one part compost, one part sharp sand, and a little added bonemeal. A more expensive variation of this mix substitutes vermiculite for the sand, producing a mix that weighs less but holds more moisture.

Potted plants should have their soil changed annually. This is a good time to place the plant in a larger container. Do not jump many pot sizes but move up one or two sizes. You will not see top growth until the roots have filled up the pots, so it's a good rule of thumb to move up in pot sizes gradually. If the root ball is tightly entwined, make a cross cut and spread out the roots to encourage additional root and plant growth.

Water

Adequate soil moisture is critical to all plants. Those in containers are especially susceptible to moisture loss as summer heat dries the soil mix rapidly. Soil in porous wood and unglazed clay containers dries out more quickly than that in plastic or other non-porous containers.

While good light and lots of sun make herbs grow into strong specimens with healthy green leaves and flowers, too much of a good thing can be harmful. If the area where your containers will be housed gets the full summer sun all day long with no shade relief, try not to use dark-colored containers, which absorb heat more readily than those made of light-colored materials. In hot sunny spells, when plants in containers are subjected to constant sun, you may need to water them two or three times a day.

In general, you'll need to water all container plants daily in hot weather, not only to keep roots moist, but to help cool your plants and wash away accumulated salts.

Fertilizer

When grown in containers, herbs need more frequent feeding than when grown in the open garden. The best fertilizer, containing all the nutrients for growth and flavor, is fish emulsion or a combination of fish emulsion and seaweed. It comes in liquid form and is readily available at garden centers and nurseries. You can also feed container herbs with homemade manure tea (see page 118 for more information).

Moving Plants Indoors

As September approaches, it's time to bring your potted herb plants indoors where they will require plenty of light and moisture. Chances are that your indoor herb garden will end up in the kitchen, and this is probably the most suitable place for it. Feed healthy, indoor herbs with liquid fertilizer every week during the summer months and once every two weeks during the fall and winter months. Trim them often and pinch out growing tips to encourage them to bush out since herbs growing indoors can get a little tall and stringy.

Remember that growth will be slower indoors as the days grow shorter. Perennials will take a break and even die back for about six to eight weeks before they start their new spring growth once again.

Preparing Outdoor Plants For Winter

Should some of your containers be too large to bring in, care must be taken in later fall to protect the less hardy plants from

---

In Rome, the bay tree was an emblem of glory. Victorious heroes and winners of games were crowned with wreaths of the leaves. Poets were garlanded with laurel leaves and this is the origin of the title "poet laureate."

risk of frost damage. The pots will need to be insulated with bales of straw or hay, and protective covering against winter winds needs to be put in place. Hardy perennials planted in above-ground pots and planters need extra protection against thawing and freezing of the soil over the winter and spring. Large planters can be grouped close to a building or barn for more protection.

In the spring, remove the protective coverings slowly, so that the soil warms up as the temperature warms up.

Strawberry Jars

There is a wide variety of plants that can be grown in a small space and are therefore ideal for growing in a strawberry jar. These include bush basil, chives, curly parsley, dill, dwarf sage, French lavender, French tarragon, nasturtiums, rosemary, scented geraniums, sweet marjoram and thyme.

The strawberry jars come in different sizes with varying numbers of pockets. The larger the jar, the more herbs can be grown and the more space will be available for the herbs' large root systems. If you're planning to use a jar with more than six pockets, you should have a PVC tube in the center in order to distribute the water to each pocket.

Cut the tube four inches shorter than the outside height measurement of the jar; drill holes in the tube at the exact levels of the pockets. Place a small screen over the drainage hole in the bottom of the strawberry jar, then secure a fine mesh screen at one end of the PVC tubing. Fill the tube with fine pebbles and secure a screen at the end when finished. The pebbles in the tube will help to distribute the water in the jar. Position the tube in the center of the jar so that the top is four inches below the lip of the jar, and begin to add your soil. There are soil options from which to choose: a combination of compost, potting soil, sphagnum moss and perlite, or a soilless mix of peat moss, vermiculite and perlite.

First, fill the strawberry jar with soil up to the bottom tier of holes. Once you've decided which plants will go in which opening, remove each plant from its container and dip its roots into a bucket of water, washing off enough soil so that the roots may be inserted into the pocket opening.

Cover the roots, making certain that the plant is firmly established in the soil. The soil level should be on an even plane with the lip of the pocket.

After planting the first tier of pockets, add more soil and continue planting the second and third tiers in the same manner. Fill the jar with soil to a point four inches below the top. As you work, cover the lower plants with a small rag to prevent soil from spilling on them.

For the top of the jar, choose a large plant that will grow in scale and proportion to the central opening. Place this plant over the PVC tube, center it, and carefully add soil all around its root system, tapping the soil (not the root ball) with the eraser end of a long pencil. Top dress the large opening with fine gravel or wood chips. This makes a neat finish and keeps the perlite from rising to the top. It also preserves moisture and prevents the foliage from being splashed with soil during watering.

Water the jar initially by soaking the bottom in a large pan of water for a couple of hours. The water level should be no higher than the bottom of the first pocket. Using a watering can, water slowly and carefully all around the top of the jar.

Keep the jar in full sun at least five hours a day and rotate it twice a week so all plants receive equal light exposure. Fertilize once a month. After a heavy rain or thorough watering, the soil will sink and additional soil may need to be added. The strawberry jar can be brought indoors in winter and put in a sunny window.

In order to grow compact plants that remain in scale, pinch the plants back frequently—a perfect reason to use your culinary herbs.

Container gardening is a way of bringing your herb plants closer to the house as well as being able to bring them indoors. Grow herbs in the ground or grow herbs in containers— whichever way suits your lifestyle.

USING
HERBS

CULINARY USES

"In my garden many herbs grow,
Along the paths to and fro:
Parsley, sage, rosemary and thyme,
All herbs for the kitchen ready to be
Used to make dishes from soup to tea."

—Rosemary Riffle,
Peoria Area Herb Guild

There's nothing quite like the fresh flavor of herbs, especially if they are grown in your own garden. Their leaves, flowers and seeds perform a bit of magic on foods with aromatic characteristics as well as with the flavor they impart. Most culinary herbs, when used as seasonings for soups and stews, stuffing, sauces, vegetables, meat and fish, will awaken your taste buds, transforming a routine meal into one of refreshing flavors and crunchy textures. Herbs add flavor to food without adding calories or fat. Some home cooks choose to eliminate salt from their diets by using fresh and dried herbs to season recipes.

Increased interest and demand for herbs for culinary use has made many varieties available year-round. Cooking with herbs has become quite convenient. Home cooks can take advantage of herbs grown outside in their own gardens or they can snip year-round from indoor pots, windowsills or strawberry jars. Plus, many grocery stores and supermarkets have responded to the demand and offer fresh herbs in their produce departments throughout the year.

There are really no "strict" rules to consider when using herbs in cooking; the best herb dishes are those you create based upon your own preference. A good way to try an unfamiliar herb on your taste buds is to snip a small amount into a bit of butter or cottage cheese. Blend mixture together then refrigerate for about an hour to incorporate the flavors. Spread on a plain cracker for tasting.

To capture the best flavor, cut fresh herbs from the garden in mid-morning. Place between two pieces of paper towel to keep dry, then place in refrigerator. Herbs will keep fresh for up to eight days.

Scissors are the best tool for snipping fresh-cut herbs into your dish or measuring cup. Dried herbs are generally about 4 times as strong as fresh: **1 teaspoon of fresh herbs equals 1/4 teaspoon of dried herbs.** Measure accordingly when converting from one form to another. Dried herbs should be stored in a covered glass jar and crumbled just before using. Frozen herbs should be measured the same as fresh and can be crumbled by hand directly into a dish. Herbs can be frozen in plastic zipper storage bags or frozen into ice cubes trays to preserve their fresh flavor for later use (see page 122 for details on preserving herbs).

When cooking, remember that herbs should enhance rather than overpower a recipe. Add in small amounts, tasting as you go. It is best to mix in the more delicate herbs during the last 5 to 10 minutes of preparing a dish so the beneficial oils which impart flavor are not cooked away.

Flavor Strength of Herbs

Herbs vary in the amount of flavor they impart. For example, you would need much less rosemary to flavor a dish than you would parsley. Rosemary has a more dominate flavor than the much milder parsley.

Dominate herbs include bay, black pepper, cardamom, hot pepper, curry, mustard, rosemary and sage. To flavor 6 servings of a dish with these herbs, use about 1 teaspoon dried herb.

Of medium flavored herbs, 1 or 2 teaspoons dried herb would flavor 6 servings. These herbs include basil, celery seed and leaves, cumin, dill, fennel, French tarragon, garlic, marjoram, mint, oregano, savory (winter and summer), thyme and turmeric.

Herbs with delicate flavor include burnet, chervil, chives and parsley. To flavor 6 servings, you would need 3 tablespoons of the dried herb. These delicate herbs work well in combination with other herbs and spices.

To flavor a dish with fresh herbs, use four times the amount recommended above.

Herb Culinary Use Chart

In cooking, herbs can be used to enhance the flavor of complementary foods or as the main ingredient to make a dish pleasingly singular. Basil, for example, is a staple in many tomato sauces, but to become more familiar with its flavor, try it in basil pesto (see page 195 for recipe).

The recommendations in this culinary use chart are a guide for both gardeners and cooks. Experiment with the herbs alone or in combination and season to your own taste.

CULINARY USE CHART

	ANGELICA	ANISEED	BASIL	BAY	BEE BALM	BORAGE	CARAWAY	CHERVIL	CHIVES	CLOVE PINKS	CORIANDER LEAVES	CORIANDER SEED	CUMIN	DILL	DILL SEED	FENNEL	GARLIC	GARLIC CHIVES	LAVENDER	LEMON BALM	LEMON VERBENA	LOVAGE	MARIGOLD (CALENDULA)	MARJORAM	MINT	OREGANO	PARSLEY	PEPPERMINT	PINEAPPLE SAGE	PURSLANE SUMMER	PURSLANE WINTER	ROSEMARY	SAGE	SAVORY	SCENTED GERANIUM LEAVES	SORREL	TARRAGON	THYME
OIL: SAVORY		●												●	●									●	●							●	●				●	●
SWEET									●										●	●																		
VINEGAR		●	●				●							●		●				●				●								●	●				●	●
MARINADE		●	●					●	●	●	●			●	●			●		●	●			●								●						
JELLY: SAVORY		●																														●	●	●				
SWEET																			●	●	●														●			
BREAD	●	●					●							●						●																		
EGG: GENERAL		●						●	●							●											●											
DEVILED		●						●	●											●		●					●											
SCRAMBLED		●														●									●	●												
CHEESE: HARD					●								●															●				●	●					
SOFT			●		●								●	●										●	●							●	●	●				
FONDUE		●														●									●													
WELSH RAREBIT		●											●														●						●					
SALAD: GENERAL	●	●			●	●	●	●	●		●		●			●		●		●			●				●	●	●			●		●		●	●	●
FLORAL			●	●			●													●																		
SOUP: GENERAL						●						●			●		●			●		●	●									●	●		●	●	●	●
MINESTRONE		●																									●											
PEA		●		●										●										●	●							●						
POTATO			●		●																						●											
TOMATO		●												●											●												●	●
VEGETABLES:																																						
ARTICHOKES		●																														●		●				
ASPARAGUS						●	●							●					●															●				
AVOCADO														●												●												
BRUSSEL SP.														●																			●	●				
CABBAGE					●	●								●									●	●	●	●							●	●				
CARROTS								●																		●												
CAULIFLOWER								●			●	●	●																			●						
CELERIAC								●																		●												
GREEN BEANS														●									●	●	●	●						●	●	●			●	●
LENTILS												●																					●	●	●			
MUSHROOMS		●									●						●			●				●								●	●				●	●
ONIONS		●																								●							●	●			●	●
PEAS		●					●																	●	●							●	●	●				

CULINARY USE CHART (continued)

	ANGELICA	ANISEED	BASIL	BAY	BEE BALM	BORAGE	CARAWAY	CHERVIL	CHIVES	CLOVE PINKS	CORIANDER LEAVES	CORIANDER SEED	CUMIN	DILL	DILL SEED	FENNEL	GARLIC	GARLIC CHIVES	LAVENDER	LEMON BALM	LEMON VERBENA	LOVAGE	MARIGOLD (CALENDULA)	MARJORAM	MINT	OREGANO	PARSLEY	PEPPERMINT	PINEAPPLE SAGE	PURSLANE SUMMER	PURSLANE WINTER	ROSEMARY	SAGE	SAVORY	SCENTED GERANIUM LEAVES	SORREL	TARRAGON	THYME
POTATOES		●	●					●						●								●		●	●	●	●					●						●
SAUERKRAUT														●								●												●			●	●
SPINACH						●	●															●	●									●				●	●	●
SUMMER SQUASH			●											●								●										●						
TOMATOES		●	●					●	●					●		●	●	●				●		●	●	●	●					●		●				●
TURNIPS														●		●						●											●					
CASSEROLES			●		●					●				●	●	●			●		●											●						●
POULTRY & GAME:																																						
CHICKEN			●					●	●					●						●				●	●								●				●	●
DUCK			●											●																		●						
GOOSE														●																		●						
TURKEY																											●					●				●	●
PIGEON																																●						
RABBIT/HARE		●	●																			●										●	●					
VENISON			●																													●	●	●				
FISH: GENERAL		●	●			●	●	●						●		●			●	●				●	●													
BAKED/GRILLED		●	●			●	●	●						●	●	●	●	●																●			●	●
OILY														●	●																							
SALMON															●																	●						
SEAFOOD		●	●					●	●					●								●										●					●	●
SOUPS			●																			●										●						
MEAT:																																						
BEEF		●	●			●	●																	●	●	●	●	●				●	●	●			●	●
HAM																					●			●	●	●	●					●	●					
LAMB			●							●												●		●	●							●	●	●				●
LIVER			●											●								●										●						
PORK								●				●			●							●										●	●	●				●
DESSERTS: GENERAL	●	●		●		●														●	●							●				●						
CUSTARD			●																							●									●			
FRUIT COMPOTE:																																						
APPLE	●						●							●																		●						
PEARS														●												●												
QUINCES																																			●			
ACIDIC FRUIT	●																																					
FRUIT SALAD:		●																		●					●		●					●						

Herbal Blends

Blended together, herbs enhance the flavor of food and, at the same time, can reduce your reliance on salt. It is worthwhile to make your own herbal blends as commercially sold seasonings found in stores often start with salt—check the label!

During the summer, blend together fresh-cut herbs, then as the end of the growing season approaches, harvest herbs for use year-round. Chop proportional amounts of herbs in the food processor with a small amount of water; place in ice cube trays and freeze. Processed herbal blends may be placed in plastic zipper storage bags and frozen.

The herbs in each of the following blends are listed in order of importance to achieve the desired result. Use larger amounts of the herbs listed at the top and gradually reduce the amount of each herb as you move to the bottom of the list. For example, add 3 or 4 tablespoons of the first herbs listed, then diminish the amount to only 1/4 teaspoon for those at the end. Certainly both fresh and dried herbs can be used in the same mixture. Remember to use 4 times as much fresh as dried.

Salad blend:	*Soup blend:*	*Poultry blend:*
basil	basil	sage
parsley	lovage	thyme
lovage	parsley	savory
marjoram	marjoram	parsley
dill	thyme	lovage
tarragon	savory	marjoram
savory	bay laurel	basil

Fish blend:	*Beef and Veal blend:*
basil	basil
lemon balm	lovage
dill	parsley
savory	thyme
rosemary	marjoram
rue	savory
fennel (leaves)	sage

Bouquet garni: a combination of bay leaves, Italian parsley, thyme and marjoram, is used to season soups, stews or braised meats. Wrap mixture in cheesecloth or place in small muslin bags. Add to pan while cooking then remove bag from pan before serving.

"Fines Herbes": a term used in French cookbooks, is a combination of Italian parsley, chervil, chives and French tarragon (fennel, oregano, sage, basil or saffron are sometimes added in small amounts). Add to sauces, especially bearnaise and hollandaise.

Herbs de Provence: the most aromatic of all herbal blends and a staple in many great French dishes. It is a blend of thyme, basil, savory, fennel, rosemary and lavender. Sprinkle on meat before cooking or grilling or use when preparing chicken.

Herb Butters

Herb butters can add some last minute seasoning to a wide variety of vegetables, breads, fish and meats. Herb butters are so versatile to use and are equally as easy to make. Always mix herbs with unsalted butter to produce the freshest flavors. Once blended, refrigerate for several hours; bring to room temperature before serving. Herb butters will keep in the refrigerator 3 to 4 weeks and can be frozen for up to 4 months.

Basic Herb Butter

4	tablespoons fresh herbs OR 1 tablespoon dried herbs
1/2	cup (1 stick) unsalted butter, softened
1/2	teaspoon lemon juice
	Dash of white pepper

In a food processor on low speed, gradually add herbs then butter. Slowly add lemon juice and pepper, mixing well. Cover and refrigerate several hours before using, to blend flavors. Butter can be stored in the refrigerator for 3 to 4 weeks or frozen for up to 4 months.

Spread on bread or rolls or serve on baked potatoes or cooked vegetables. Butter is also good melted over prepared chicken, fish or steak.

Makes 1/2 cup

Outstanding Herb Butter

1 cup (2 sticks) unsalted butter, softened
1 tablespoon finely chopped fresh green basil
1 tablespoon finely chopped fresh marjoram
1 tablespoon finely chopped fresh chives
1 teaspoon finely chopped fresh rosemary
1 teaspoon lemon juice

Make butter 1 or 2 days before serving so flavors will blend. In a medium bowl, using a wooden spoon, blend butter, basil, marjoram, chives, rosemary and lemon juice. Cover and refrigerate. Butter can be stored in the refrigerator for 3 to 4 weeks or frozen for up to 4 months.

Serve on baked potatoes or hamburgers. Use for toasting sandwiches or melt over prepared meat and fish.

Makes 1 cup

Herb Butter for Chicken

1 cup (2 sticks) unsalted butter, softened
3 cloves garlic, finely chopped
2 tablespoons chopped fresh rosemary leaves
1 tablespoon chopped fresh Italian parsley
2 teaspoons finely grated lemon peel
   Salt and pepper, to taste

In a food processor combine butter, garlic, rosemary, parsley, lemon peel, salt and pepper. Mix to blend. Cover and refrigerate several hours before using, to blend flavors. Butter can be stored in the refrigerator for 3 to 4 weeks or frozen for up to 4 months.

Baste chicken with herb butter several times while baking.

Makes 1 cup

Herb Butter for Fish

1/3 cup minced fresh parsley

2 green onions, minced

1/2 cup chopped fresh dill

2 tablespoons chopped fresh tarragon

1 tablespoon chopped fresh chervil

1 cup (2 sticks) unsalted butter, softened

2 tablespoons lemon juice

Salt and pepper, to taste

In blender or food processor combine parsley, onions, dill, tarragon, chervil and butter. Add lemon juice, salt and pepper and blend well. Refrigerate for several hours to blend flavors; bring to room temperature before using. Butter can be stored in the refrigerator for 3 to 4 weeks or frozen for up to 4 months.

Use to baste fish while broiling or melt butter and serve with prepared fish for dipping.

Makes 1 cup

❦

Herb Jelly

In mid-winter when the evenings draw in and dinner is eaten with lights on, bring to mind the joy of a bountiful summer of herbs by serving herb jellies. They not only looks enticing, with herbs and flowers suspended in clouds of pink, orange, yellow, red and green, but they taste excellent too. Herb jellies create unusual flavors when basted on beef or lamb roasts, chops, ham or chicken. Herb jellies can also be used as a glaze for a fresh fruit tart and to make Herb Jelly Thumbprint Cookies (see page 206 for recipe). Flower jellies go great with whole grain breads, scones, biscuits, ice creams and puddings.

Late summer is the best time of the season to make jellies. This is when the essential oils, which give herbs their distinct taste, are at their peak. The most easily made herb jellies are based on an herbal infusion or flavor saturation. Jellies can feature a single flavor or a combination. However, flavoring with a single herb is a good way to get to know the taste of that herb; plus, it gives you an idea of which foods it marries with best. Any edible herb can be used, but those with the strongest flavor yield the most distinct jelly.

Today, with more emphasis on health and natural sweeteners, pectins such as Sur-Jell Light and Slim Set allow sugar amounts to be reduced in the jelly and cooking time to be decreased from 45 minutes to about 4 minutes. Some recipes call for powdered pectin but you can substitute liquid pectin by following package directions. Jelly made with pectins may appear paler in color, but they still retain a fruity herbal taste.

Since some pectins, herbs or herb combinations can cause jelly to be a dull color, choose a complimentary color of food coloring to create visual appeal. Add several drops of coloring during the cooking process (see page 181 for recipe). Use clear containers and always sterilize them before adding jelly.

Jellies can be put in decorative glass jars, cups or glasses; cover with colorful fabrics and ribbons to make a nice gift for any occasion.

Some individual herbs to try are: anise hyssop (licorice mint), applemint, chocolate mint, lavender, lemon balm, lemon verbena, orangemint, oregano, pineapple sage, rose geranium, rosemary, savory and thyme.

Certainly there are combinations of herbs that will spark your taste buds, too. Some of these may whet your appetite:

Apple juice* with lavender, mint, oregano and/or oregano blossoms, rose petals, sage, scented geraniums or thyme. (*If you use fresh-pressed apple juice, there is no need to add pectin since it contains natural pectin.)

Grapefruit juice with anise hyssop, calendula petals, marjoram, mint, parsley or tarragon.

Orange juice with basil, lavender, rosemary or thyme.

Pineapple juice with chives, cilantro, garlic, parsley, pineapple sage, sage or thyme.

Red wine or red grape juice or currant juice with garlic, rosemary, savory or thyme.

White wine or white grape juice with dill and/or dill blossoms, lemon geranium, lemon grass, pink rose petals, sweet woodruff or tarragon.

Basic Herb Jelly Recipe

3 cups unsweetened apple juice, canned or bottled
1 cup packed herb leaves and flowers,
     twisted and bruised to release oils
1 package Sur-Jell powdered pectin OR Sur-Jell Light
4 cups sugar
   Several drops of food coloring

Combine apple juice, leaves and flowers, and pectin in nonreactive pot (coated or enamel). Bring to hard rolling boil for 5 minutes. Turn off heat, let cool for 10 minutes, then strain out herbs and flowers.

Add sugar, stirring to dissolve; continue stirring and add food coloring. Bring to a second rolling boil for about 2 minutes. Turn off flame, allowing foam to rise to the top. With a slotted spoon, skim off foam in a few quick passes. Pour into sterilized jars and seal.

Makes 5 jars, 8 ounces each

Herb Vinegars

Preserving herbs in the form of vinegar will provide many flavorful pleasures in the kitchen long after fresh herbs have been snipped from the garden. Herb vinegars make anything that can be prepared with plain vinegar taste better without adding fat, salt or calories. There is no end to the combination of herbs and spices that will add new flavor to your salads, vegetables, main dishes and desserts. Pickles and relishes will take on new personality, too.

There are a variety of vinegars that you can begin with. The quality and flavor of vinegar varies greatly. It is not necessary to purchase a premium vinegar since a medium priced vinegar is usually of sufficient character to make a good flavored vinegar. Do not use distilled vinegar as it just does not work. Many people prefer vinegars that are made from organic sources or that are unfiltered and unpasteurized, as more care and attention often go into the manufacturing process. The advantages of pasteurizing are that bacterial activity is curtailed and quality is more consistent. No matter what vinegar is selected to start with, it is important to like it before making the herb vinegar.

Home-grown herbs, freshly picked, will yield the best results. The time to pick is between 9 A.M. and 11 A.M. to get the best in flavor and essential oils. Be sure to gather a nice handful, using about one cup of herbs to two cups of vinegar. Once picked, rinse under cool water and pat dry with paper towels. Be sure to select leaves that will look good in the bottle, those with no holes or spots.

There are two methods for making herb vinegar: cooked and uncooked. For both, have all ingredients ready before beginning, including herbs and sterilized glass bottles. As an option, once the vinegar is ready, the herbs can be strained out to preserve clarity. A convenient way to strain herbs and flavoring particles is to pour the vinegar through a coffee filter, such as a Melitta brand filter. Then, using a funnel, pour clear vinegar into decorative sterilized bottles. You may also add a fresh, unbruised herb sprig to the bottle for flavor identification and decoration.

Make sure that the bottles you select have lids that are not metal. Cork, plastic, ceramic or glass will not change the flavor as metal has a tendency to do.

If you use corks, it's nice to seal the bottle with wax and ribbon. Cut a long piece of ribbon, and tie it in a knot around the neck of the bottle. Bring the two ends of ribbon over the top of the cork and down the other side. Turning the bottle upside down, dip it in hot paraffin wax several times. This will seal the cork and prevent leakage. The bottle can be dipped in wax to cover 2 to 3 inches from the top. Leave some of the ribbon loose so that it can be pulled to open the bottle. It is fun to add a recipe written on a small card tied around the neck of the bottle. This also gives a nice finishing touch, especially if you are giving the vinegar as a gift.

Be sure to label the bottles with either your own labels or ones purchased at housewares or kitchen supply stores.

Unopened bottles will last a year. It is a good practice to date the bottle when you open it. Use vinegars within three to six months of opening.

Herbs that can be used for flavoring vinegars include: all basils, bay, borage, chervil, chives, dill, fennel, garlic, garlic chives, lavender, lemon balm, lemon grass, lemon verbena, lovage, marjoram, oregano, parsley, rose geranium, rosemary, sage, salad burnet, savory, spearmint, tarragon and all thymes.

Herb vinegar combinations:

Apple cider vinegar:

-Basil, whole cloves, garlic and whole cracked nutmeg

-Bay, dill, and garlic

-Chives, garlic, lemon balm, shallot and tarragon

-Dill, garlic, lemon balm and mustard seeds

-Horseradish, hot pepper, and shallot

Champagne vinegar:

-Lemon balm, lemon thyme and lemon verbena

-Lemon grass and lemon zest

Red wine vinegar:

-Basil, bay, garlic, rosemary, sage and savory

-Basil, garlic, oregano, and black peppercorns

-Bay, cilantro, hot red peppers, rosemary and sage

-Borage, burnet and dill

-Burnet, lemon balm and marjoram

-Fennel, garlic, hyssop, oregano, rosemary and thyme

White wine vinegar:

-Basil, fennel, garlic, and parsley

-Whole cloves, elderflowers, garlic, lemon balm, peppercorns, spearmint and tarragon

-Cilantro, garlic, oregano and hot red pepper

-Lemon balm, lemon basil and mint

-Basil, chervil, chives, savory and tarragon

Uncooked Method

Cut herbs and select starting vinegar. Measure twice as much vinegar as herbs—for example, 1 cup of herbs to 2 cups of vinegar. Gently place herbs in sterilized bottle, twisting and slightly bruising the leaves to release oils. Add vinegar to cover herbs. Once bottle is filled, seal it with a nonmetal lid.

Place bottle in a sunny location, turning it each day to cure. In about two weeks, uncork bottle for a test sample. If it is to your liking, store in a dark place at room temperature until ready to use. If you prefer a stronger flavor, continue to steep the herbs for up to a month. Place in a dark place at room temperature once it is to desired strength.

Whether the original herbs are left in the bottle or they are strained out is all a matter of preference. Replace with fresh herbs for decoration and identification.

Cooked Method

Cut herbs and select starting vinegar. Measure twice as much vinegar as herbs—for example, 1 cup of herbs to 2 cups of vinegar. Bruise and twist herbs to release oils; place herbs in sterilized bottle. Heat vinegar to boiling; pour over herbs to cover. Close bottle tightly with a nonmetal lid. Let steep overnight. Strain out herbs; place vinegar back in bottle. Place a fresh, unbruised sprig of herbs in vinegar bottle for decoration and identification.

Besides herbs, you can use spices, fruits, flowers and vegetables in numerous combinations to flavor vinegars.

Herb Oils

Herb oils are a wonderful way to enjoy the fresh flavors of herbs with your favorite foods. There are a variety of uses: marinate meats and cheese, toss with pasta or simply drizzle over bread. They can be used to season a salad or spice up marinades. For a subtle, delicious flavor, marinate fish and vegetables with flavored oil. Herb-flavored oils help prevent grilled foods from burning while bringing out their fresh flavors. Vegetables, fish and meat can be basted before or during the cooking process. For additional herbal flavor, baste foods with a brush made of fresh-picked herbs (see page 188 for instructions).

The most common all-purpose oils are made with basil, rosemary, oregano, citrus-flavored herbs and garlic. You can experiment with different combinations of herbs and use them in varying amounts to satisfy your own taste. For additional flavor, herbs can be left in the oil when using or removed to make an infused oil.

When making herb oils, use a good-quality olive oil. Select extra-virgin, which contains oil of superior quality olives pressed out in the first cold press. It contains no cholesterol and less than 1% acidity. Extra-virgin olive oil has a light and delicate taste and a clear greenish color.

Unlike vinegars that store indefinitely in the pantry, oils must be stored in the refrigerator. Homemade oil tends to become rancid once opened, therefore it is best to make in smaller quantities. (The recipes found on pages 186-187 call for 1 quart of oil. These recipes can easily be cut in half.) Also, take care to cover all of the herbs and other ingredients in the container with oil to prevent mold from developing. Remember, always start with sterilized bottles or jars.

To prepare, bruise fresh herbs by twisting or pressing to release oils. Place herbs and seasonings into sterilized bottles or jars. Add extra-virgin olive oil and cover tightly. Store in a cool, dark place for 10 days. Refrigerate; when chilled, oil will thicken and appear solid. Remove from refrigerator about 1 hour before using in order to liquefy.

Fish Oil

For marinating and broiling fish.

3	dried fennel stalks	1	tablespoon coriander seeds
2	sprigs dill	1	teaspoon black peppercorns
3	sprigs lemon thyme		Zest of 1 lemon
3	sprigs parsley	1	quart extra-virgin olive oil

Bruise herbs to release oils. Place fennel, dill, thyme, parsley, coriander, peppercorns and zest in a sterilized 1-quart container. Pour in oil, making sure all ingredients are completely covered. Cover tightly and store for 10 days in a cool, dark place. Refrigerate until ready to use. Bring oil to room temperature 1 hour before using.

Marinate fish up to 4 hours in a shallow baking dish with enough oil to cover bottom of dish. Turn occasionally. For broiled fish, baste each side of fish while cooking.

Spicy Oil

Use for stir fry or to marinate pork or chicken.

2	small hot, dried chilies	1	teaspoon coriander seeds
2	cloves garlic	1	teaspoon whole allspice
4	slices gingerroot, 1/4-inch thick		Zest of 1/2 orange
1	cinnamon stick	1	quart extra-virgin olive oil
1	star anise pod		

Place chilies, garlic, gingerroot, cinnamon, anise, coriander, allspice and zest in a sterilized 1-quart container. Pour in oil, making sure all ingredients are completely covered. Cover tightly and store for 10 days in a cool, dark place. Refrigerate until ready to use. Bring oil to room temperature 1 hour before using.

To stir fry, place 3 tablespoons oil in a heated wok. When oil is hot, add chopped vegetables or cubed meats. Cook to desired doneness.

To marinate pork or chicken, place enough oil to liberally cover bottom of a baking dish. Add meat and turn to coat. Marinate up to 4 hours, turning occasionally.

Herb de Provence Oil

For marinating, sauteing or grilling meats or marinating cheeses.

3 sprigs rosemary
2 sprigs thyme
2 cloves garlic
3 sprigs marjoram
3 sprigs oregano
2 stems basil
3 bay leaves
6 black peppercorns
1 quart extra-virgin olive oil

Bruise herbs to release oils. Place rosemary, thyme, garlic, marjoram, oregano, basil, bay leaves and peppercorns in a sterilized 1-quart container. Pour in oil, making sure all ingredients are completely covered. Cover tightly and store for 10 days in a cool, dark place. Refrigerate until ready to use. Bring oil to room temperature 1 hour before using.

To marinate beef, lamb, pork or chicken, place enough oil to liberally cover bottom of a baking dish. Add meat, turning to coat. Marinate for up to 4 hours.

To marinate cheese, place in jar and cover with oil. Store in refrigerator until ready to use or for as long as 7 days.

To saute meats, coat bottom of a heavy skillet with oil. Turn heat to medium-high. When oil is hot, add meat and saute until desired doneness. To grill meats, baste both sides while cooking.

Herb Basting Brushes

To baste roasts, fish and vegetables.

Herb basting brushes can be dipped in flavored oils, regular olive oil or butter for basting. When making the brush, choose fresh herbs that will complement the flavors of basted foods. A brush made of sage is ideal for basting chicken, turkey and beef. Thyme complements chicken, pork and beef. Rosemary can be used when basting chicken, lamb or beef. Dill is wonderful for fish.

1	wooden dowel, 6-inches long, 1/8 to 1/4-inch diameter
1	handful-size bunch of herbs, 3 to 4 inches in length
1	rubber band
3 to 4	strands natural raffia

Push dowel through center of herbs so end of dowel is even with cut stems. Wrap rubber band tightly around stems and dowel. Trim ends of stems if desired, so all stems are flush with end of dowel. Push bundled herbs down length of dowel to form a handle. Wrap raffia over rubber band and fasten into a bow or knot. Dip leaves in flavored oil to baste meat and vegetables.

❧

Herbal Teas

Herbal teas are rich in herbal symbolism—mint for wisdom, thyme for bravery, calendulas for good complexion and disposition, rosemary for remembrance, chamomile for quiet sleep and sage for immortality. Whether or not tea is made for these reasons, the promise of a good cup is certainly enough of an incentive to grow herbs to make tea. Growing your own plants also allows you to enjoy teas of superb quality, guaranteed free of sprays or foreign matter. For the most part, growing your own plants is a wonderful way to experience their freshest flavor since some leaves are too delicate to survive drying.

Tea can be made from fresh, dried or frozen herbs. It tastes best when brewed in an earthenware tea pot because it stays hot for a longer period of time.

To Dry Herbs For Tea

Cut stems with leaves and flowers in the mid-morning for maximum flavor. Make into small bunches of no more than eight stems and rubber band together at the cut end. Poke holes in a brown lunch bag for ventilation; put herbs in bag. The bag protects leaves from dust and dirt in the air. Gather open end of the bag around rubber-band end of the herbs. Secure bag and stems together with string or rubber band.

Hang upside down in a well ventilated area for approximately 2 weeks. Hot and/or dry weather is ideal for drying; damp and/or cool weather will slow the process. Remove from bag; strip the leaves and flowers off stems and store in an airtight container. For the best flavor crumble herbs just before using. Dried leaves and flowers will keep about a year.

When preparing tea, use one tablespoon dried crushed leaves per cup of water. Pour boiling water over leaves and let steep 5 to 10 minutes. Strain out leaves and flowers before serving.

To Make Tea With Fresh Herbs

Pick leaves and flowers in the mid-morning to retain flavors. Use four tablespoons of crushed leaves and flowers per cup of tea. Pour boiling water over the leaves and let steep 5 to 10 minutes. Strain and drink hot or make into iced tea.

To Freeze Herbs For Tea:

Fresh-picked herbs can be frozen to make tea at any time of the year. In order to preserve herbs for tea, chop up the leaves and flowers; place in ice cube trays. Add boiling water then place tray in freezer. Once frozen, remove from tray and store herb cubes in plastic zipper storage bags. Toss 1 cube per cup (or more, based on desired strength) in a pot of boiling water to release flavor. Steep for 5 to 10 minutes. Strain out leaves and flowers before serving.

Suggestions For Herbal Teas:

There is nearly an unlimited selection of organically grown herbs, flowers and berries for making refreshing and healthy teas.

The mint family is probably the most familiar and popular. Varieties include spearmint, peppermint, black peppermint, applemint, orange mint, English mint, bergamot mint and on and on. Teas can be made from one mint or by blending several kinds for a unique flavor. Leaves can be used fresh or dried, although dried is slightly less flavorful than fresh.

Another very popular tea is German chamomile; its blossoms have a sweet, fruity flavor. Chamomile is considered a calming herb for the stomach and nerves. With chamomile, generally use only the flowers.

For a lemon flavor, try lemon balm. To get an enjoyable fragrance and flavor, use only the leaves. Lemon balm tea is good hot or iced.

The many varieties of basil make unusual teas. Use sweet basil, purple basil, lemon basil, anise basil, and especially cinnamon basil, which has a more spicy flavor. Pick and use both the leaves and the flowers. Try blending other herbs with basil to make tea. For example, combine cinnamon basil with hibiscus flowers, lemon balm and blackberry leaves.

Garden sage is considered a winter tea, good for colds and sore throats. Add honey and lemon to sooth the throat or to enhance the flavor. When drying for winter tea, use both the leaves and flowers.

Pineapple sage has the flavor and aroma of fresh pineapple. The leaves can be used fresh or dried and are ideal blended with other fruit-flavored herbs such as hibiscus, rose hips, lemon balm, lemon grass or chamomile. Pineapple sage leaves make a tropical flavored tea.

Anise hyssop has both beauty and flavor. This plant has violet blue flowers with licorice mint flavored leaves. Anise hyssop tea is delicious hot or over ice. Tea can be mixed with lemonade. Try combining fresh anise hyssop leaves and flowers with hibiscus flowers for a flavorful hot or iced tea. Capture the full flavor of this herb by using both the fresh flowers and leaves.

Soups

Lemon Balm Soup

4 cups chicken stock	4 tablespoons lemon juice
1/4 cup long grain rice	3 tablespoons finely chopped lemon balm
3 eggs	Freshly ground black pepper

Combine stock and rice in a stock pot. Place over medium-high heat and bring to a boil. Cover, reduce heat and simmer until rice is tender, about 20 minutes.

In a medium bowl beat eggs; mix in lemon juice. Add 1 cup of stock drained from pot of cooked rice; stir well. Turn heat to low and whisk mixture into rice mixture. Continue whisking until soup lightly thickens, taking care not to let soup curdle by boiling. Add lemon balm and stir to combine. Season with pepper. Serve hot.

4 to 6 servings

Chervil Nasturtium Soup

2 quarts water	1 pound potatoes, peeled and quartered
1/2 teaspoon salt	1 cup heavy cream
2 cups fresh chervil	1 tablespoon butter
1 cup nasturtium leaves	Nasturtium leaves, for garnish
1 cup watercress leaves, large stems removed	

In a large pot, bring water to a boil over high heat. Add salt, reduce heat to medium-low, and add chervil, nasturtiums, watercress and potatoes. Simmer gently for 1 hour.

Puree soup ingredients in a food processor or blender in batches. Return to pot and reheat over low. Stir in cream just before serving. Place butter in bottom of a tureen or serving bowl and pour hot soup over it. Garnish with nasturtiums, if desired.

8 servings

Fresh Tomato Soup with Basil Dumplings

For soup:

- 1/4 cup olive oil
- 2 large onions, sliced
- 2 shallots, minced
- 2 cloves garlic, minced
- 2 carrots, peeled and finely diced
- 2 ribs celery, diced
- 1 sweet red pepper, seeded and diced
- 2 tablespoons lemon juice
- 1 teaspoon sugar
- 3 cups chicken stock
- 3 pounds ripe plum tomatoes, peeled, seeded and diced
- 1 tablespoon gin

For dumplings:

- 1 cup flour
- 1 teaspoon baking powder
- 1/2 teaspoon salt
- 3 eggs
- 2 tablespoons vegetable oil
- 3/4 cup torn fresh basil leaves, divided
- Salt and freshly ground black pepper, to taste

Heat olive oil in a large stock pot. Add onion, shallots and garlic. Saute over medium heat for approximately 5 minutes, stirring occasionally. Add carrots, celery, red pepper, lemon juice, sugar and stock. Simmer for 15 minutes.

Strain out vegetables, returning stock to pot. Puree vegetables in a food processor or blender; return to stock pot. Add tomatoes and gin. Simmer for 10 minutes, or until soup begins to thicken. Watch carefully to prevent soup from burning.

To make dumplings, combine flour, baking powder, and salt in a large bowl. Add eggs and oil; beat until dough is sticky. Stir in 1/2 cup of the basil.

Bring a large pot of water to a rapid boil. Drop dough by 1/2 teaspoons into boiling water. Simmer dumplings uncovered for 3 to 4 minutes after they rise to the surface. Turn periodically to cook through evenly. Test for doneness by removing a dumpling and checking the center to be sure it is cooked through.

Drain dumplings in a colander. Rinse under cold water and drain again. Just before serving, add dumplings to soup to heat through. Add salt and pepper to taste. Garnish soup bowls with remaining 1/4 cup basil.

4 to 6 servings

Breads

Rosemary Biscuits

2 cups whole wheat flour
2 cups unbleached white flour
1/2 teaspoon salt
2 teaspoons baking powder
1 teaspoon baking soda
1 tablespoon sugar
4 tablespoons unsalted butter
2 tablespoons fresh rosemary, chopped fine
   OR 2 teaspoons dried rosemary, crumbled
11/2 cups milk

In a large bowl sift flours, salt, baking powder, baking soda and sugar together. Cut in butter to make pea-sized lumps. Add rosemary and milk; mix together to form a soft dough.

Preheat oven to 400 degrees. Grease and flour a baking sheet. Roll dough to 1/2-inch thickness on a lightly floured board. Cut into 11/2-inch squares. Place squares close together on prepared pan. Bake for 20 minutes. Serve hot, or remove to racks to cool.

Makes 24 to 36 biscuits

------ ❦ ------

*Sicilian fairies made their homes
under large rosemaries and rocked
their babies in the rosemary flowers.*

Country Herb Twist Bread

1 envelope active dry yeast	2¹/2 to 3 cups all-purpose flour
1 teaspoon sugar	1¹/2 teaspoons salt
1/4 cup warm water (110 degrees)	2 tablespoons minced fresh oregano
2 tablespoons unsalted butter, divided	2 tablespoons minced fresh thyme
1 cup water	2 tablespoons minced fresh rosemary

In a large bowl, sprinkle yeast and sugar over warm water; stir to dissolve. Let stand until mixture becomes foamy.

Melt 1 tablespoon of the butter. Add to yeast mixture with 1 cup water. Combine 2¹/2 cups flour and salt; stir into yeast mixture 1/2 cup at a time, to form a slightly sticky dough. Add up to 1/2 cup additional flour if necessary.

Turn dough out onto a lightly floured surface and knead until smooth and elastic, about 5 minutes. Lightly butter a large bowl; place dough in bowl and turn to coat entire surface. Cover bowl with a cloth and let rise in a warm draft-free area until doubled in volume, about 1¹/2 hours.

Punch dough down. Divide dough into thirds. Turn out 1/3 onto a lightly floured surface and knead in oregano. Shape dough into a rope by rolling between the palms of the hands. Roll to 20 inches long, tapering the ends of the rope. Set aside. Repeat the rope-shaping process using another 1/3 of the dough, and kneading in thyme. Repeat process with remaining 1/3 dough, kneading in rosemary.

To braid, arrange the 3 dough ropes side by side. Starting at the middle and working toward one of the ends, braid ropes together, pressing them into a point at the tapered ends. Turn the bread; again braid the ropes from the middle to the end, pressing the tapered ends in the same manner. Transfer bread to a buttered baking sheet. Cover loosely with a clean cloth and let rise in a warm place or until doubled in volume, about 45 to 50 minutes

Preheat oven to 375 degrees. Melt remaining 1 tablespoon butter. Brush loaf with butter and bake for 20 to 30 minutes, or until top is golden and loaf sounds hollow when bottom is tapped. Let cool on a rack for 30 minutes before serving.

Makes 1 large loaf

Pesto Bread

1½ envelopes active dry yeast	Yellow or white cornmeal,
2 cups warm water (105 to 115 degrees)	for the baking sheet
1½ teaspoons salt	1½ cups Basil Pesto
1 tablespoon sugar	(see below for recipe)
6 to 7 cups all-purpose flour	

In a large bowl, dissolve yeast in water and add salt and sugar. Stir thoroughly. Set aside briefly until foamy.

Using a wooden spoon, beat in flour, one cup at a time, until a smooth dough forms. Turn out on a lightly floured board and let rest a few minutes, then knead until the dough is elastic, about 5 minutes. Place in a lightly oiled bowl, cover with a towel, and set in a warm, draft-free place until doubled in volume, about 1½ hours.

Turn dough out onto a lightly floured board, punch it down and knead again. Divide the dough in half. Pat out two rectangles, each about 10x12 inches, and spread a thin layer of pesto mixture over each, leaving a 1-inch border. Starting with a long side, roll each rectangle of dough into a cylinder and shape into a loaf. Allow loaves to rise for 5 minutes.

Sprinkle a baking sheet with cornmeal and place the loaves on it. Brush each loaf with cold water and place in a cold oven. Place a pan of boiling water in bottom of oven and turn oven to 400 degrees. Bake bread for 35 to 40 minutes, or until the loaves are browned and sound hollow when tapped. Place bread on a rack to cool slightly and serve warm for the greatest flavor.

Makes 2 loaves

Basil Pesto

2 cups fresh basil leaves	2 cloves garlic
½ cup parsley leaves	1 teaspoon salt
½ cup olive oil	½ cup freshly grated Parmesan cheese

Puree basil, parsley, oil, garlic, and salt in a blender or food processor. Stir in cheese. Store any leftover pesto in refrigerator with a thin layer of oil on top, or freeze.

Makes 1½ cups

Herb Bread Sticks

3   cups all-purpose flour
1   envelope rapid-rise dry yeast
1   tablespoon salt
1/4 cup chopped fresh parsley
1   bunch fresh chives, chopped
2   tablespoons chopped fresh dill
7   tablespoons olive oil
6   tablespoons very warm water (130 degrees)
    Cornmeal

In a large bowl, mix flour, yeast, salt and herbs. Add olive oil and water, and mix until a dough is formed. On a floured surface, knead dough until smooth and elastic, about 5 minutes. Place dough in an oiled bowl, cover with a towel, and set in a warm place to rise. When dough has doubled in size, about 30 minutes, punch it down and divide it into 16 pieces. Roll each piece into a 12-inch "snake."

Sprinkle 2 sheet pans with cornmeal. Transfer bread sticks to the sheet pans, cover with dish towels, and leave in a warm place to rise for about 20 minutes.

Preheat oven to 400 degrees. Bake until lightly browned, 15 to 20 minutes.

Makes 16 bread sticks

Sage Bread with Green Olives

For sponge:	20	large green olives
4 envelopes active dry yeast	30	fresh large sage leaves
2 cups warm water (110 degrees)	7½	cups all-purpose flour
2 cups plus 1 tablespoon	2	cups warm water (110 degrees)
all-purpose flour, divided	1	teaspoon salt
Pinch of salt	½	teaspoon freshly ground black pepper

Start sponge the night before baking or at least 10 hours ahead of time. In a small bowl, dissolve yeast in water, stirring with a wooden spoon. In a large bowl place 2 cups of the flour and make a well in center. Pour dissolved yeast and salt in the well; with a wooden spoon, gradually mix until flour is incorporated. Sprinkle top of dough with remaining 1 tablespoon of flour; cover bowl with a cotton dish towel. Place bowl in a warm place away from drafts; let rest at least 10 hours or overnight.

Pit olives and cut into ½-inch pieces. Tear sage leaves into small pieces. Set aside.

Mound flour on a bread board or work surface. Make a well in the center of the mound and place sponge in well. Pour water over sponge and begin incorporating a small amount of surrounding flour with your hands. Continue mixing in small amounts of flour from the mound until dough thickens and becomes batter-like. Add salt, pepper, olives and sage to batter and use hands to mix in flour from the rim of the well. When about 1 cup of flour remains, begin kneading the dough in a folding motion with palms of hands to incorporate the remaining flour. Knead about 10 minutes or until dough is smooth. Shape into a long loaf and place on a floured kitchen towel. Wrap towel loosely around loaf and place in a draft-free warm place until double in size, about 1 hour.

Line middle or bottom shelf of oven with oven-proof unglazed terracotta tiles or a pizza stone. Preheat oven to 400 degrees.

When dough has doubled in size, remove from towel and immediately place in hot oven directly on stone or tiles. Bake for about 1 hour and 15 minutes or until crust is hard and loaf sounds hollow when tapped on the bottom. Cool for at least 3 hours before slicing.

Makes 1 loaf

Main Dishes

Tiny Pasta with Ten Herbs

3	teaspoons chopped fresh Italian parsley
3	teaspoons chopped fresh basil
2	teaspoons chopped fresh chives
2	teaspoons chopped fresh chervil
1	teaspoon chopped fresh tarragon
1	teaspoon chopped fresh sage
1	teaspoon chopped fresh oregano
1	teaspoon chopped fresh marjoram
1	teaspoon chopped fresh thyme
1	teaspoon chopped fresh rosemary
1/2 to 3/4	cup extra-virgin olive oil
2	cloves garlic, peeled and finely chopped
1/2	teaspoon red pepper flakes
	Salt and freshly ground black pepper, to taste
1	pound tiny shaped pasta (such as tripolini or other small pasta)
	Freshly grated Parmesan cheese, optional

In a medium saucepan, combine parsley, basil, chives, chervil, tarragon, sage, oregano, marjoram, thyme, rosemary, olive oil, garlic and pepper flakes. Turn heat to low; using a wooden spoon, gently stir until herbs turn bright green, releasing their fragrance, about 2 to 3 minutes. Season with salt and pepper to taste.

Cook pasta according to package instructions or until al dente. Drain, leaving some moisture clinging to pasta; place in a warm serving bowl. Pour herb mixture over pasta and toss, adding salt if desired and several grindings of coarse black pepper. Serve immediately with an optional sprinkling of Parmesan cheese.

4 to 6 servings

Pork Loin Roast with Herbs and Glazed Apples

2 tablespoons balsamic vinegar

2 tablespoons dry sherry

1 tablespoon olive oil

1 tablespoon shoyu* OR soy sauce

1 tablespoon cracked black peppercorns

2 sprigs (about 3-inches each)
   fresh rosemary

2 sprigs (about 3-inches each)
   fresh marjoram

2 sprigs (about 3-inches each)
   fresh thyme

2 cloves garlic, minced

2 pork tenderloins (about 2/3-pounds each),
   trimmed of fat and membrane

2 tablespoons vegetable oil
   (preferably canola)

   Salt, to taste

4 Gala, Golden Delicious or other
   cooking apple

2 tablespoons unsalted butter or margarine

1 sprig (about 3-inches) fresh sage

1/4 cup bourbon

2 tablespoons honey

* Shoyu is a sweet soy sauce made from toasted wheat.

To marinate, combine vinegar, sherry, olive oil, shoyu OR soy sauce, peppercorns, rosemary, marjoram, thyme and garlic in a shallow glass baking dish. Add pork turning to coat; cover with plastic wrap. Place in refrigerator for 1 to 4 hours, turning several times. Remove from refrigerator 20 minutes before cooking to bring to room temperature.

Preheat oven to 425 degrees. Heat vegetable oil in a large skillet over medium heat. Remove tenderloins from marinade; place in skillet and brown pork on all sides, about 2 minutes per side. Place pork in a glass or cast-iron roasting pan; pour marinade over meat; add salt if desired. Place pan uncovered in oven and roast until internal temperature reaches 150 degrees, about 20 minutes. Strain pan juices and reserve.

Core apples and slice into 1/4-inch thick rings. Melt butter in same skillet over medium-high heat. Add apples and sage; cook until apples begin to brown lightly, about 5 minutes, turning occasionally. Add bourbon and honey. Continue cooking until apples are almost translucent, another 10 minutes. Remove sage sprig.

Place pork on a serving platter; surround with apple rings. Pour reserved sauce over meat. Cut pork into 1-inch thick slices and serve immediately.

6 servings

199

Baked Salmon Noel

1 whole salmon (4 to 6 pounds)	Sorrel leaves, for garnish
4 tablespoons olive oil	Lemon slices, for garnish
Freshly ground black pepper, to taste	Parsley sprigs, for garnish
4 to 6 cups sorrel leaves, washed	

Preheat oven to 350 degrees. Remove head of fish; clean cavity. Wash well and pat dry. Lay salmon on a large piece of aluminum foil. Brush skin with oil and season inside with pepper. Stuff cavity with sorrel leaves then cover outside with remaining leaves. Wrap salmon tightly in foil.

Place fish in a baking pan and bake for 1 hour. When fish is done, it should flake, yet be firm and moist. Test for doneness and bake for an additional 10 to 15 minutes if necessary.

Remove pan from oven; unwrap fish and discard sorrel leaves. Place fish on a warm platter; garnish with sorrel leaves, lemon slices and sprigs of parsley. Serve with Sorrel Sauce (see below for recipe) and lemon butter.

8 to 10 servings

Sorrel Sauce

2 cups sorrel leaves, washed
1¼ cups chicken stock OR fish stock
1 tablespoon butter
1 tablespoon flour
¼ cup half-and-half
Freshly ground black pepper, to taste

In a small saucepan cook sorrel leaves in stock for 5 minutes. Place mixture in a blender or food processor; puree until smooth.

Over medium heat melt butter in a skillet. Add flour, whisking constantly to form a roux. Slowly add pureed sorrel, whisking constantly until well-blended. Simmer mixture over low heat 4 to 5 minutes. Add cream and pepper; stir to combine. Continue to whisk until sauce is heated through.

Makes 3 cups

Apricot Rosemary Chicken Baked in Parchment

4   tablespoons unsalted butter, divided
2   whole chicken breasts, boned, skin removed
4   fresh apricots, cut in half and pitted*
2   ounces prosciutto, finely minced
2   sprigs fresh rosemary, lightly bruised
1   teaspoon chopped fresh sage
1   clove garlic, sliced paper-thin
    Salt and freshly ground black pepper, to taste
    Juice of 1 lemon

* If fresh apricots are not available, use dried apricots
  soaked in white wine for 30 minutes.

Preheat oven to 350 degrees. Cut two circles of parchment paper about
18 inches in diameter. Spread 1 tablespoon of the butter on top of each circle.
Place a chicken breast on one half of each parchment circle.

Thinly slice apricots. Arrange equal amounts of apricots, prosciutto,
rosemary, sage and garlic over each chicken breast. Sprinkle with salt and
pepper to taste. Dot breasts with remaining 2 tablespoons of butter. Squeeze
lemon juice over each breast. Fold parchment in half over chicken; crimp
edges to seal. Place packets on baking sheet and bake for 45 minutes.

Remove from oven and place on serving plates; break open packets and
serve immediately.

2 servings

Leg of Lamb Roasted on a Bed of Rosemary

  6   whole garlic bulbs, unpeeled
  1   leg of lamb (about 5 pounds)
  2   cloves garlic, peeled and cut into slivers
 1/4 cup olive oil
      Salt and freshly ground black pepper, to taste
 12   large sprigs fresh rosemary
  6   Italian plum tomatoes, sliced crosswise
  2   tablespoons lemon

Place garlic bulbs in a saucepan. Add enough water to cover and parboil for 5 minutes. Drain and set aside to cool.

Make slits in lamb with point of a knife. Insert garlic slivers into slit areas. Brush lamb and garlic bulbs with olive oil. Sprinkle lamb with salt and pepper.

Preheat oven to 400 degrees. Put rosemary sprigs and tomatoes in a shallow roasting pan. Place lamb on rosemary and tomatoes; surround with garlic bulbs. Squeeze lemon juice over lamb.

Roast uncovered 1 hour for rare meat, or longer to desired doneness. Remove from oven; place lamb on a carving board and let rest for 10 minutes. Remove rosemary sprigs from roasting pan. Return pan to oven to keep tomatoes and garlic warm.

Carve lamb into thin slices; arrange on heated serving plates. Spoon pan sauce over slices and place a garlic bulb on each plate. Garlic pulp can be squeezed from skins and eaten plain or spread over lamb slices.

6 servings

Desserts

Scented Geranium Cake

24 scented geranium blossoms
   (a few small leaves can be used)
6 extra-large eggs
   plus 4 extra-large egg yolks
2 cups sugar
2 1/2 cups unbleached white flour

1/2 teaspoon salt
1 cup unsalted butter, melted
   Zest from 1 lemon
   Rose Geranium Flavored Sugar
   (see below for recipe)

Preheat oven to 375 degrees. Generously butter and lightly flour a 13x9x2-inch baking pan. Arrange geranium flowers on bottom of baking pan.

Combine eggs, yolks, and sugar in large bowl of an electric mixer. Beat ingredients until batter is pale yellow and very thick, about 5 minutes

In a separate bowl sift flour and salt three times. Slowly fold about one-third of flour mixture into egg mixture; repeat with remaining two-thirds. Carefully fold about one-third of melted butter into batter; repeat with remaining two-thirds butter. Fold in lemon zest.

Carefully pour batter into pan over flowers. Place cake in center of oven and bake until the top is light golden-brown about 35 to 40 minutes. Check for doneness with a tester, taking care not to overbake.

Remove cake from oven and cool 15 minutes on wire rack. Run a knife around edge of cake; invert pan onto the wire rack and cool completely. Place cake on a serving platter and lightly sprinkle cake with Rose Geranium Flavored Sugar. Serve plain or with whipped cream. If desired, garnish with a bouquet of fresh geranium flowers and leaves.

10 to 12 servings

Rose Geranium Flavored Sugar

24 fresh scented-geranium leaves
1 cup sugar

In a glass jar, place leaves in between layers of sugar. Cover jar tightly. Set aside for 24 hours for sugar to absorb oils from leaves. Sprinkle sugar on cakes and cookies.

Lavender Ice Cream

2 tablespoons finely chopped fresh lavender leaves

2 tablespoons sweet white dessert wine
   (such as muscat, sauterne or monbazillac)

21/2 cups heavy cream

7 tablespoons Lavender Flower Flavored Sugar
   (see below for recipe), divided

2 egg whites

2 tablespoons fresh lavender flowers

In a small bowl stir lavender leaves into wine; let rest in a warm place for 10 minutes for flavors to infuse. Strain wine; discard leaves.

In a medium bowl beat cream until stiff peaks form. Gradually add wine and 31/2 tablespoons of the flavored sugar.

Beat egg whites in a small bowl until stiff peaks form. Mix in remaining 31/2 tablespoons of the sugar. When blended, fold into cream and wine mixture. Carefully stir in lavender flowers. Place in container and freeze until firm. To serve, scoop into sherbet or ice cream dishes.

6 to 8 servings

Lavender Flower Flavored Sugar

24 fresh lavender flowers

1 cup sugar

In a glass jar, place flowers in between layers of sugar. Cover jar tightly. Set aside for 24 hours for sugar to absorb oils from flowers. Sprinkle sugar on cakes and cookies.

Lemon Tea Bread

3/4 cup milk	1 1/2 teaspoons baking powder
1 tablespoon finely chopped fresh lemon balm*	1/4 teaspoon salt
1 tablespoon finely chopped fresh lemon thyme*	6 tablespoons butter, at room temperature
1 tablespoon finely chopped fresh lemon verbena*	1 cup sugar
2 cups flour	2 eggs
	1 tablespoon grated lemon zest

* Use any combination of lemon herbs

Preheat oven to 325 degrees. Butter a 9x5x3-inch loaf pan.

In a medium saucepan heat milk and herbs until just below boiling point. Remove from heat and let steep until cool.

Mix together flour, baking powder, and salt in a medium bowl; set aside.

Using an electric mixer, cream butter in a large bowl; gradually add sugar. Continue beating until mixture is light and fluffy. Beat in eggs one at a time. Add lemon zest. Alternate adding flour mixture and herb milk. Mix until batter is just blended.

Spread batter into prepared pan. Bake for about 50 minutes, or until a toothpick inserted in the center comes out dry. Place a sheet of wax paper under wire rack; remove loaf from pan and place on rack. Pour Lemon Glaze (see below) over hot loaf. Decorate with a few sprigs of lemon thyme.

Makes 1 loaf

Lemon Glaze

3 tablespoons fresh lemon juice

1/2 to 3/4 cup powdered sugar

Put lemon juice in a bowl and add sugar, stirring until a thick but still pourable glaze forms. Drizzle over hot bread.

Herb Jelly Thumbprint Cookies

21/2 cups flour

11/2 teaspoons baking powder

1/4 teaspoon salt

1 teaspoon cinnamon

1 cup sugar

3/4 cup vegetable oil

2 eggs

1 teaspoon vanilla

1/2 cup Herb Jelly (see page 181 for recipe)

In a small bowl sift together flour, baking powder, salt and cinnamon.

Cream sugar and oil in a medium bowl with an electric mixer. Add eggs one at a time, beating well after each addition. Mix in vanilla. Add flour mixture all at once, beating until well-blended.

Preheat oven to 375 degrees. Roll dough into 1/2-inch balls; place on lightly greased or parchment-lined baking sheet. Slightly flatten balls with thumb. Place a dab of jelly in thumbprint. Bake 10 to 12 minutes.

Makes 5 dozen

Sage Apple Cake

2 cups unbleached white flour

1 teaspoon baking soda

1 teaspoon baking powder

1/2 teaspoon salt

1/2 teaspoon cinnamon

1 cup plus 3 tablespoons brown sugar

3/4 cup plus 2 tablespoons unsalted butter, at room temperature

2 large eggs

1 tablespoon minced fresh sage

1 cup Sage Honey Applesauce (see page 208 for recipe)

1 large McIntosh, winesap or other good cooking apple

1 tablespoon lemon juice

In a medium bowl sift flour, baking soda, baking powder, salt and cinnamon. Set aside.

In a separate bowl, cream 1 cup of the brown sugar with 3/4 cup of the butter. Beat in eggs. Blend sage into applesauce and add to creamed mixture, beating well. Gradually add flour mixture, blending ingredients until well combined.

Preheat oven to 350 degrees. Peel apple, core and slice thin. Toss slices with lemon juice. Butter bottom and sides of a 9 1/2-inch bundt pan with remaining 2 tablespoons butter. Sprinkle bottom and sides of pan with remaining 3 tablespoons brown sugar. Arrange apple slices around bottom and sides of pan.

Pour batter carefully into prepared pan. Bake for 50 to 60 minutes, until top is a deep golden-brown and a cake tester comes out clean. Cool cake on a rack for 15 minutes. Loosen sides of pan and invert cake on a wire rack to cool completely. Place on serving platter.

10 to 12 servings

Sage Honey Applesauce

6 large McIntosh apples (about 2 pounds)

1/2 cup light honey

2 sage leaves

1 to 2 tablespoons lemon juice

Peel, core and coarsely chop apples. Place in a heavy saucepan; stir in honey, sage leaves and lemon juice. Cover and cook over low heat for 30 to 40 minutes, until apples have softened. Remove pan from heat and discard sage leaves. Puree apple mixture in a food mill or food processor.

Let sauce cool to room temperature. Store covered in refrigerator until ready to serve.

Makes about 2 cups

❧

DECORATING
& GIFT IDEAS

As a gardener there is nothing more rewarding than to be able to bring all of the intensely fragrant herbs and flowers inside to be enjoyed all year long. There are so many ways to use herbs to make decorative items for the home or to give as gifts. Whether for a wedding, holiday centerpiece or a relaxing bath, use herbs to provide a natural, beautiful and inexpensive way to make it special.

Potpourris

Walking into a room filled with the rich scent of a beautiful potpourri is aromatherapy at its best. The term "potpourri" means a mixture of dried flowers, herbs and spices all scented with rich oils to add fragrance to a room. A true potpourri smells absolutely wonderful and can keep its scent for a very long time.

For those who love fresh flowers, herbs and spices, making and using potpourri allows enjoyment of their fragrance and beauty the year round. Displaying bowls of potpourri is like leaving little presents all around the house. Potpourri has a wide varieties of uses—in cushions, sachets, tussie mussies, flower baskets, soaps and even in bath water.

The art of making potpourri is ancient, going back to the Middle Ages. During the Victorian era it was very common to find a bowl of potpourri in the bedroom, the sitting room and the library. Today you can buy potpourri, but it is more fun to make it using the flowers and herbs from your own garden. There is no mystery involved in making potpourri, it is as easy as following a cooking recipe.

The traditional potpourris contain five groups of ingredients: scented flowers and petals, woods, roots or barks; herbs and leaves; spices; fixatives; and essential oils. Dried berries and dried fruits or seed heads can be added for color and appearance.

Scented Flowers and Petals, Woods, Roots and Barks: Pick perfect, whole flowers just before they are fully open. Dry by laying as flat as possible on stretched cheesecloth to allow air to circulate. Large-flowered roses and thick petaled lilies and hyacinths should have their petals separated. Small rosebuds can be dried whole.

Some popular flowers to choose from are: carnations, freesias, honeysuckle, hyacinth, jasmine, lavender, lilac, meadowsweet, mock orange, narcissus, nicotiana, orange blossom, roses, stocks, violets and wall flowers.

Woods, roots and bark are also aromatic additions to your potpourri. Shreds of cedarwood, sandalwood or cassia chips are excellent potpourri enhancers.

Herbs and Leaves: Not to be overlooked, leaves and herbs have a scent that is often more powerful than that of flowers. Dry leaves whole, then crush them to release their scent. Choose from basil, bay, bee balm, lemon balm, lemon verbena, mints, scented geraniums, rosemary, sage, southernwood, sweet marjoram, sweet woodruff, tarragon, thymes and wild strawberry.

Spices: These have a strong aroma and are used sparingly—about one tablespoon of spices to four cups of flowers and leaves. The best scent is obtained by freshly grinding whole spices in a pestle and mortar.

You can select from allspice, aniseed, cardamom, cinnamon, cloves, coriander, dill seed, ginger, nutmeg, star anise, vanilla pods, dried peel of citrus fruits, roots of angelica, cowslip, sweet flag and valerian.

Fixatives: These are available as powders and are used to absorb and hold the other scents so they last longer. The most popular vegetable fixative is orris root, as its sweet violet scent does not strongly affect a blend. Fixatives can be purchased at craft stores. Use one tablespoon per cup of flowers and leaves.

Essential Oils: These are concentrated vital essences of aromatic plants. They add intensity and depth to a fragrant mixture. Oils are good for reviving a potpourri that has lost its scent, but remember that they must be used with discretion to avoid dominating subtler scents. Essential oils can be purchased at craft stores.

Flowers for Color: To give your potpourri a little added color, mix in bee balm, borage, calendula, cornflowers, delphinium, feverfew, foxglove, larkspur, poppy, sage, tansy, tulip petals or zinnias.

Mixed Leaf and Herb Potpourri

1   cup dried eucalyptus leaves
1   cup dried bay leaves
1   cup dried lemon verbena leaves
1/2   cup dried uva-ursi (bearberry) leaves
1/2   cup dried rosemary
1/2   cup dried thyme

1/2   cup dried sage
A few whole sprigs dried thyme
1/2   cup powdered orris root
Several drops of lime, vervain
or rosemary essential oil

Put eucalyptus, bay, lemon verbena, uva-ursi, rosemary, thyme, sage and thyme sprigs in a large enameled bowl. Add orris root and mix well with hands or a wooden spoon.

Add several drops of oil, stirring continuously. Put mixture into sealed containers or jars. Leave in a cool, dark place to cure for several weeks before using.

Rose and Mint Potpourri

1   teaspoon cinnamon powder
1/2   teaspoon ground mace
2   tablespoons orris root powder
3   drops rose oil
2   drops rosewood oil
1   drop lemon oil

1/2   teaspoon whole cloves
4   cups dried rose petals and blooms
2   tablespoons dried mint leaves
2   tablespoons dried lavender
Additional dried whole rose blooms

In a small bowl, mix cinnamon, mace, orris root powder, oils and cloves.

In a separate bowl, mix dried flower petals, leaves and lavender.

Pour orris root mixture over flowers and mix thoroughly with hands to ensure mixture is evenly distributed throughout potpourri.

Place potpourri in an airtight container or covered jar and leave in a dark place for at least six weeks. Shake container every day for first week.

After six weeks, transfer potpourri to a decorative bowl and adorn the top with reserved rose blooms.

Lemony Kitchen Potpourri

1/4 cup dried rosemary

1/2 cup dried bay leaves

2 cups dried lemon verbena

3 3-inch cinnamon sticks, crushed

1 cup dried lemon balm

1 tablespoon whole cloves

2 tablespoons dried cardamom pods

Peel of 2 lemons, dried and cut in 1/2-inch pieces

1/4 cup dried sunflower petals

6 drops lemon oil

2 drops bay oil

1 tablespoon orris root chips

Combine all ingredients in a large enameled bowl. Place potpourri in an airtight container or covered jar. Cure in a dark, cool place for about six weeks. Stir or shake every few days.

❧

Sachets

Sachets are wonderful little items to tuck around the house just about anywhere you'd like to add a touch of fragrance. They can be put in closets, drawers, blanket chests, armoires or desks; tie them on furniture or place them behind pillows on beds and sofas. In the late eighteenth century women even wore perfumed sachets in the folds of their long, billowy skirts. Sachets make terrific gifts, too, especially if you have made them yourself.

There are so many kinds of sachets, made by using different bags and different potpourris. To make a very elegant bundle, take a linen handkerchief with lace edging, put several tablespoons of potpourri in the center, bring up the ends and tie it with pastel ribbon.

You can also make sachet bags with some pretty printed natural fabrics such as cotton, linen, silk or muslin. A pouch can be easily sewn on the sewing machine or you can just cut a square, trim the edges using pinking shears, fill the center and tie it closed with ribbon. Antique fabric scraps like small quilt pieces or bits of Victorian silk can be made up into truly beautiful sachets. Pieces of handmade lace, old or new, lined with batiste or tulle in soft pastel colors will add that special touch.

Once you've gathered your fabrics and ribbons, you'll need to decide what kinds of sachets to make. It doesn't matter if the ingredients of a sachet mixture get crushed in the blending because it will be hidden in the bag.

To make a sachet, mix ingredients in a glazed pottery bowl. Put mixture in a brown paper bag lined with wax paper and store in a cool, dark place to age for a period of two weeks. Occasionally stir contents with a wooden spoon to disperse blended oils.

When mixture has cured, spoon it into fabric bags and tie with ribbon.

Lavender Sachets

6 tablespoons dried lavender flowers
2 tablespoons powdered orris root
4 drops lavender oil

Travel Sachets

Change the smell of musty hotel rooms—
hang on doorknobs, tuck into drawers and closets.

2 tablespoons dried rose petals
2 tablespoons cinnamon sticks, crushed
2 tablespoons powdered allspice
2 tablespoons cut oak moss
2 tablespoons dried rosemary sprigs, crushed
1 tonka bean, crushed
2 drops bergamot oil

Lemon Furniture Sachets

*For an English lemon wax scent, tie bags on bedposts or chairs
or tuck behind a shelf of books.*

2 tablespoons dried lemon verbena leaves
2 tablespoons dried lemon balm
2 tablespoons dried lemon thyme
2 tablespoons cut lemon peel
2 tablespoons dried chamomile flowers
2 tablespoons cut oak moss
4 drops lemon verbena oil

Moth Sachets

*Great for tucking into blanket chests, sweater drawers
or putting on a hanger in storage closets.*

1/4 cup dried southernwood
1 tablespoon whole cloves
2 tablespoons cedar shavings
2 tablespoons powdered orris root
2 tablespoons cut oak moss
2 cinnamon sticks, crushed

Powdered Sachets

Perfect for linen closets.

1/2 cup cornstarch or unscented talcum
10 drops of your favorite rich, floral essential oil such as
tuberose, magnolias, hyacinth or jasmine.

Herbal Bath Sachets

*Several minutes before getting into the tub, swish one of these bags around
in the hot bath water to scent it. Afterwards, hang the bag from the faucet
until the next time. Each sachet is good for several baths.
It is best to use unbleached muslin tied with twine.*

Flower Petal Sachet

2 tablespoons rose petals
2 tablespoons dried lavender flowers
2 tablespoons rolled oats (for bulk)
2 tablespoons cut orange peel
2 tablespoons cut lemon peel
2 dried bay leaves, broken
2 dried sprigs rosemary, crushed

Lemony Bath Sachet

4 cups dried lemon verbena
2 cups dried thyme
1 cup dried peppermint

The length of time a sachet's fragrance will last depends on where it is used. Sachets placed in a closed drawer or chest will last longer than those tied onto a hanger in a closet. When a sachet fades, you can revive it with a gentle squeeze or pour the contents of the bag into a bowl, add a few drops of the essential oils, cure for a few days, then return contents to the sachet bag. Occasional pep-ups of your bags will allow them to be fragrant for years.

Dream Pillows

Long before the advent of inner spring mattresses, bedding was stuffed with a variety of aromatic grasses. This rather lovely idea eventually led to the creation of herb pillows. For centuries it has been known that certain herbs, smells or evocative odors will affect dreams. Certain herbs under the pillow were believed to protect one from evil, while other herbs were used to calm bad dreams, illicit good dreams or quiet restlessness.

Today there is considerable evidence that pleasant fragrances do have a positive effect on dreaming. Some bring forth the dreams of fancy. Other herbs cause us to remember our dreams, while still other herbs help us to relax and sleep. The principle is simple—fragrances cause our brain to be stimulated in certain ways. It's the same principle that aromatherapy uses—smells evoke certain responses in people, sleeping or awake.

Possibly you have received a bouquet of fresh flowers, placed it on your nightstand, then experienced widely evocative dreams. You may have experienced the pleasant effects flowers blooming under your open bedroom window have had on your dreams.

A dream pillow is the dried version of flowers and herbs growing outside your bedroom window. It is a small bag or sachet made of cloth and filled with herbs that have a history of use in stimulating dreams. The sachet or bag can be tucked inside the pillowcase, or it can be put inside a small decorative pillow made especially for that purpose. The dream pillow should be placed where you will gently smell the subtle fragrances as you sleep.

Dream pillows should hold from one-half cup to one cup of herbs. To contain the herbs, make a bag from open weave cotton cloth in colors and prints conducive to relaxing. Cut two pieces of cloth four inches across and seven inches long. Sew three sides of the cloth to make a bag that is approximately three inches across and six inches long. Fill the bag with one of the dream blend recipes or make your own. Tie the bag with ribbon or string.

———————————— ॐ ————————————

"A bag to smell unto, or to cause one to sleep."

—Ram's Little Dodoen, 1606

*Put dried rose leaves in a glass jar—separately crush
mint leaves and crush cloves—both to a powdered state.
Mix the powders with the rose leaves, put in a cotton
bag. Take the bag to bed with you and it will cause you
to sleep, and it is good to smell at other times.*

Pleasant Dreams Blend

This is a relaxing, soothing mixture.

1 cup dried mugwort
1/2 cup dried rose petals
1/3 cup dried chamomile
1/3 cup dried lavender
1/3 cup dried catnip
2 tablespoons dried mint

Combine mugwort, rose petals, chamomile, lavender, catnip and mint in a bowl. Place mixture in a paper bag and close. Set aside for one week to allow fragrances to blend. Use 1/2 cup in cotton bag tied with string.

Action-Packed Dream Blend

1/4 cup chopped, fresh pine needles
1/2 cup dried mugwort
4 dried marigold blossoms, crushed
1 small cinnamon stick, crushed
4 whole cloves
1 cup dried rose petals
1/2 cup dried lavender

Combine pine needles, mugwort, marigold, cinnamon, cloves, rose petals and lavender in a bowl. Place mixture in a paper bag and close. Set aside for one week to allow fragrances to blend. Use 1/2 cup in a cotton bag tied with string.

If you have dried herbs from summer, you can combine a custom blend. Some pleasant dream herbs to try are fresh balsam fir needles, chamomile, dill seed or leaf, hops, lavender and sweet woodruff. Other herbs and plants that work well are clover, lemon grass, marjoram, mints, mugwort, mullein leaves, fresh pine needles, rose leaves, rose petals, rosemary, sage and thyme.

Dream herbs are not potpourris. Don't use potpourri in a dream pillow as the results may be unpleasant. Commercial potpourris are made with synthetic fragrance oils that are not recommended for long-term breathing. It is best to use the dried plants and not the oils.

Pleasant dreams!

───────────────── ❧ ─────────────────

There are a number of fresh flowers that have varying but pleasant effects on many people's dreams. Some of the fresh flowers that affect dreams are: gardenia, lavender, lilac (old-fashioned garden variety), rose (especially "honey-bells" variety), tuberose, jasmine, magnolia, hyacinth, narcissus, parma violet and honeysuckle.

Lavender Wands

When lavender is in bloom you can smell its heady fragrance throughout the garden. And when you think of the pleasures dried lavender can bring during the cold months of winter, it spurs you to find the time to make lavender wands. They are a charming old-fashioned way to enjoy the scent of lavender wherever you put a wand.

These wands take a bit of patience, but they are worth the effort.

> 19   fresh lavender stalks, cut as long as possible
> 4   feet of 1/4-inch ribbon

Strip leaves from lavender stalks. Tie stalks together just below heads. Holding flower heads in your fist, bend stems down from the point where they are tied back over flower heads. Secure stalks temporarily with a rubber band. Stalks should be evenly spaced and form a little cage around flowers.

With ribbon at top of cage, drop one end of ribbon through cage and let it hang. Take the other end of ribbon and, starting at the top of cage, weave ribbon in and out through stalks until flowers are completely enclosed. Remove rubber band. Wrap ribbon around stems several times and then, using both ends of ribbon, tie a knot and a bow. Trim ends of the ribbon and stalks to even lengths.

Place lavender wands in linen or lingerie drawers or keep on top of the dresser for its beauty and scent.

Natural Dyes

Many of us only think of preserving as it pertains to canning and freezing the bountiful harvest from our gardens. Preserving can also be in the form of natural dyes from your garden or from the woods.

Throughout history, dyes, stains and colors made from plants have been used for a variety of purposes. The blending that takes place to create naturally dyed material is the same way color blends in nature. Look at the color of the grass as it blends with that of the trees. For those with a love of color, there is something primitively satisfying about taking weeds destined for the compost pile and re-routing them into your dye pot.

Flowers are considered traditional dye plants; these are easy-to-grow annuals and perennials that make lovely additions to your landscape or cutting gardens. But herbs too can make wonderful dyes. Some of the more common flowers and herbs to grow in your garden and use for dying are:

African daisies	Garlic	Red bud
Agrimony	Indigo	Rosemary
Asters	Iris	Sage
Columbine	Marigolds	Salvia
Coneflowers	Mint	Southernwood
Cosmos	Pansies	Sunflower
Dill	Parsley	Tansy
Evening primrose	Poppies	Yarrow

Materials collected from the wild can be used for dyes too; some of them may surprise you.

Barberry twigs and roots—strong yellow dye

Bindweed or creeping jenny—dull green to khaki to yellow

Black walnuts (soak hulls and boil)—black

Coltsfoot—greens and yellowish greens

Dandelion (flowers, stems, leaves and roots)—yellows and greens

Dock (seeds, leaves, flowers)—beige to brown to green

Elderberry bush (leaves, bark and berries)—greens, black, purple-blue or pink beige

Goldenrod (flowers)—rusty orange

Grapes (leaves and fruits)—yellows and blues

Milkweed (leaves and flowers)—moss green to yellow to brown

Mullein (leaves and stalks)—yellows and golds

Mustard (flowers)—brilliant shade of yellow

Stinging Nettle (whole plant)—creamy beige to yellow

Oak (bark)—black or yellow

Pokeweed (berries)—dark purple

St. John's Wort (stems, leaves, flowers)—bright yellow

Sumac (berries, stems, leaves, twigs)—brown, yellow, gray and black.

With some exceptions, there are strong seasonal trends in particular plants. In the spring, soft colors such as yellow and chartreuse greens are predominate. As summer comes and goes, these same plants produce colors in the warmer range of gold, bright orange and reddish orange. With winter comes the browns, tans and beiges. Gather your dyes at different seasons to increase color possibilities.

Just as there is a best time for planting certain plants, there is also a best time for harvesting dye materials. Flowers can be enjoyed right up until the time they begin to fade and then should be plucked one by one and saved for the dye pot. Berries and fruits, like grapes, sumac and blackberries, should be picked when ripe. Nuts should be collected as soon as they fall to the ground. Roots are best when gathered in the fall. Barks and tree roots are best gathered between February and June, when they produce the most intense color. To avoid damaging the trees, collect bark from the ground, from firewood or from prunings of tree limbs.

Collect dye plants, twigs and leaves in a large porous paper bag, which allows the materials to "breathe." Plastic bags ruin the materials by trapping moisture and causing mold and mildew.

Place materials being used as dyes in a large enamel pot of boiling water and allow to steep for 24 hours. Strain out the dye materials and bring the liquid back to a boil. Remove pot from the heat and put items to be dyed in the liquid. The longer you leave them in the liquid, the deeper the color will be.

All natural fibers can be dyed with natural dyes. This includes cottons, wools, embroidery flosses, linens, silks and even basketry fibers. Protein fibers such as wool or silk dye easily. The plant or vegetable fibers such as cotton, linen, jute and raffia can be dyed with natural dyes, but it takes a bit more work. Use your dyed fibers in decorating, needlework, knitting, crocheting and rug hooking.

Herbal Bouquets

As the cooler weather approaches, it's time to preserve the wonderful aromas of your herb garden to fill the house. The bouquets can be made fresh and allowed to dry naturally to enjoy all winter. As long as the arrangement is placed in a room with good air movement it will dry naturally without losing any flowers.

I prefer to make most herbal arrangements with fresh herbs because they are easier to work with and certainly more pliable. And, of course, the more you twist and bend the stems, leaves and flowers, the greater the scents.

Herbal bouquets can be made from a wide variety of flowers and herbs. It's best to gather herbs with stiff stems such as anise hyssop, borage, lavender, lemon verbena, marjoram, oregano, rosemary, sage, scented geraniums, thyme or anything else you desire. By allowing some of your herb plants to flower, you will be able to enjoy them visually as well as aromatically.

A fresh herb bouquet or posey makes a very pretty arrangement to stand in a vase or to be tied with ribbon and given to a special friend.

Kitchen Herb Bunches

Fresh herb bunches hanging in the kitchen are pretty simply as decorations. Always harvest the herbs when there is no moisture on the leaves or petals and before mid-day, when their volatile oils and, therefore, their scent are at their strongest. Make small bunches and tie them with colorful ribbon or raffia.

Hang the bunches in a warm, airy part of the kitchen to dry. Hanging them from wood dowels, vine hooks or unusual wire drying racks works well.

Once dried, you can freshen the scent by misting with warm water or by rubbing or bruising the leaves.

Wreath/Centerpiece

Making an herbal wreath or a circular centerpiece can be done using the same equipment and method. Both are made on a circular wreath form of either wire, styrofoam or straw.

In order to help you determine the amount of material needed, consider that an 8-inch wire form takes one pound of fresh herbs to make a 14-inch finished centerpiece; a straw or styrofoam form takes half as much. Fresh herbs are easier to work with than dried because they are bendable and won't crumble. Be creative: wire, glue or wrap bunches of your herbs and flowers around the form and arrange in a circular fashion. If using wire to attach bunches, a #24 or #26 cloth-coated wire works well; it can be purchased at craft stores.

I like to make the wreath on a thin wire wreath form. For a 14-inch finished wreath on a wire form, you will need to make 21 handful-size bunches of fresh herbs and dried flowers with the stems three to four inches long. When making the bunches, there should be some stems longer than others for the overall effect.

All 21 bunches can be the same or you can make three different groups of seven each. It's best to put a rubber band around each bunch, because as it dries, the stems shrink and it will loosen if not secured. Once all of the bunches are made, you can start to wire each bunch onto the wreath form, starting around the circle and angling the bunch outward.

When finished, this will stay fresh for about 10 days. Let it dry naturally. When you want to refresh the smell of fresh herbs, just mist with warm water. The dried wreath will last indefinitely. Use a hair dryer to blow away any accumulated dust.

The centerpiece is breathtaking with a fat candle in the center.

Holiday Gift Ideas

To most people, Christmas brings thoughts of pine and fir, juniper, holly and mistletoe. But to those who love herbs, Christmas is a time when their pleasure in these fragrant greens and colorful flowers can be shared with herbal gifts and aromatic decorations to delight friends and family.

Herbs are mixed with evergreens in wreaths and swags, fashioned into old-time kissing balls and shaped into trees and tree decorations. Turn herbs into centerpieces for the holiday table, and make them into potpourris and pomanders to scent the home or to give to a friend.

Fresh Rosemary Christmas Tree

This 12-inch Christmas tree is made from sprigs of rosemary and can be used as a dramatic centerpiece as well as a focal point on a table in your entryway.

To make this, you will need:

1 pound fresh rosemary, cut into 3- to 4-inch sprigs
2 blocks of floral oasis for fresh flowers, standard size 8 inches tall
  Curved plastic dish that can hold water

Stand blocks of oasis next to each other vertically. Put a stick through the center to hold the two pieces together and, with a knife, shape blocks like a Christmas tree. Place floral oasis in the dish and wet it.

Beginning at the bottom and going around floral oasis, push in sprigs of rosemary at 45 degree angles, working up to the top. When finished, water again, then decorate with rose hip berries, small ornaments or strings of cranberries.

Your rosemary Christmas tree will stay fresh longer by watering it daily and keeping it in the refrigerator at night.

Pomander Balls

Prior to the nineteenth century, women made all of the medicinals, cosmetics and scents for the home. All of the ingredients for their blends were kept in a "still room." This very important room in the house was where the herbs, leaves, spices, barks, berries, roots, grasses and flowers were gathered after they were dried.

Mixtures of these ingredients were blended into pungent smelling botanicals that were placed around the home to add a magical fragrance to the air. There is an old-fashioned quality about mixing and blending scents for the home that make them so very special.

Some of these smells can be enjoyed in the form of cinnamony pungent pomanders piled high in bowls. These smells add a soothing fragrance throughout the house as well as a bit of old world charm.

Pomander balls are fruits—oranges, apples, lemons and limes—studded with cloves and allowed to cure in a spice mixture. The wonderful spice-rich aroma they emit is a quick spirit-lifter. Because they look and smell so festive, pomanders have long been a holiday tradition. But their use is not limited to the holidays—they can be used year-round.

You can pile mounds and mounds of them in bowls all by themselves or mixed with potpourri. You can even try piling the pomander balls on a bed of dried lavender or dried rosemary. They can be tied with a beautiful ribbon and hung from a chandelier or in a doorway. If you make lots of them, you can hang them in closets or linen cupboards. They'll not only scent everything, they'll also help to repel moths (another virtue of cloves).

Making pomander balls can be a family project and is an ideal way to introduce children to the fun of working with herbs and spices. It's a great project for a rainy day.

To make pomander balls, you will need firm, thin-skinned oranges, apples, lemons and limes; whole, large-headed cloves for a visual effect as well as a good, strong smell; and a thin metal crochet hook or knitting needle for piercing the fruit (this makes it easier and saves your fingers).

Prepare a curing mixture of:

> 1/2 cup powdered cinnamon
> 1/4 cup powdered cloves
> 1 tablespoon powdered allspice
> 1 tablespoon powdered orris root

Blend curing mixture in a small bowl.

Make your pomander balls by poking holes in fruit with your needle and inserting whole cloves close together, covering the entire piece of fruit. Sprinkle half of mixture in bottom of a large bowl and place studded pomanders on top. Sprinkle remaining curing mixture over pomanders. Each day, turn pomanders and sprinkle them with spice mixture. Continue until pomanders are hardened. This can take from two weeks to a month. When hardened, they are ready to display. Store curing mixture in a plastic bag between uses; mixture can be used over and over again.

Pomanders should never be discarded. They just shrink slightly with age. To renew their fragrance, dampen pomander by dunking quickly into a bowl of warm water. Place balls in a bowl of curing mixture and cover bowl with plastic wrap. Turn balls each day for several weeks. You may also add a drop of essential oil such as cinnamon, allspice, or clove if desired. Your pomanders should be as good as new.

Fruit and Herbal Centerpiece

This centerpiece is made by stacking three antique glass cake stands into a tiered display filled with fruit and herbs, topping it off with a tall glass for more height. Each tier of the centerpiece can be piled with pomander balls along with a mixture of unadorned lemons, limes, apples, tangerines, bunches of grapes, pears, persimmons and even small grapefruit. Sit a single pomander in the mouth of the glass of the top tier.

This is yet another way to use your studded pomanders, or make some special orange pomanders by scoring designs in the peels (use naval oranges as they are easier to work with) and filling in these designs with whole cloves. Designs can be rows, circles or any decorative pattern you choose. Since these will not be cured, you may want to make them only several days ahead and keep in the refrigerator until ready to use.

Leaves from whatever herbs that are available from your garden or from indoor plants can be tucked among the fruits for additional fragrance and color. Herbs with body, such as bay laurel, rosemary, sage and thyme, work well. Sprigs of evergreens, rose hip berries, pepperberries and cranberries can also be used. Top off your centerpiece with long graceful strips of orange peel curling like festive streamers draped over the pomander in the glass.

This assortment of fruits and greenery can also be piled in wooden bowls and placed on the fireplace mantle or on your buffet. If you want it to stay fresh throughout the holiday season, put the green herb sprigs in fresh flower tubes with water.

Fireplace Bundles

While you are cleaning up your garden for the winter, collect dried branches of lavender, rosemary, thyme and any other herbs. Tie them together in bundles with colorful string or raffia and put them in a basket near the fireplace. Add dried flower for a little color in your bundles.

On those cold days when you come in to warm up by the fireplace, toss a bundle on the embers to release their pleasant scents.

Fireplace bundles make great gifts too—fill a basket with bundles tied with colorful cord to be enjoyed at holiday gatherings.

The Smell of Christmas

I usually have this mixture, or one like it, in the oven from Thanksgiving to Christmas. Its wonderful spicy aroma fills the house with Christmas.

2 to 3 tablespoons whole cloves
4 to 5 cinnamon sticks
1 to 2 tablespoons whole allspice
1 whole nutmeg, coarsely chopped
Piece of vanilla bean, if available
Peel from 1 to 2 oranges, fresh

Combine all ingredients in an old pan with a loose fitting lid. Add water to cover ingredients. Cover pan and place in oven set at 200 to 250 degrees. Keep mixture wet by adding water to the pan. After several days of brewing, it's best to throw away the mixture, clean the pan and start over.

Christmas Potpourri

This special potpourri calls for one gallon of dried evergreens. Some of the best greenery to use is spruce, juniper, cedar and arborvitae. Collect small pieces of evergreen and lay on an old window screen to dry; the drying process will take a week or two.

1 cup fixative (cut cellulose, reindeer moss or oak moss)
10 to 20 drops of cinnamon oil
1 gallon dried evergreens
1 quart small pine cones (hemlock is perfect)
1 cup dried orange peel
1/2 cup whole cloves
1 cup broken cinnamon sticks
1/2 cup whole allspice

Place fixative in a large jar; add cinnamon oil and shake well. Put on lid and let soak for a day. Add evergreens, pine cones, orange peel, cloves, cinnamon sticks and allspice. Colorful dried flowers can be added. Put potpourri in bowls throughout the house and enjoy the fresh smells of the season.

Gifts for Gardeners

As Christmas approaches, we scurry about looking for special gifts for gardening friends and family members because, of course, gardeners are extra special. Gifts made from your garden or related to the new gardening season will be greatly appreciated.

Be creative with your gift choices; put together gifts that have long-lasting remembrances, fragrances and flavors. Seeds make a wonderful addition to a gardener's gift basket. Seeds are living gifts that send a message of renewal and faith in the future. You will have the satisfaction of giving a gift that provides not only present pleasure but a long season of growth and harvest. Consider giving unique seed collections such as those for growing old-fashioned everlasting flowers.

Create your own gifts using a terra-cotta plant pot and filling it with gardening items such as seeds, scissors, gloves, fertilizer, gardener's soap, hand salve and whatever else you can find that makes it a personalized gift.

Find a great flower-gathering basket and fill it with some of your homemade herb jellies, pesto, chutneys and any other items that were canned from your garden. There is a sentimental feeling attached to giving a gift created from your garden. Personal handmade gifts come from the heart. Tie ribbons around the neck of bottles and jars with the recipe attached. We always want to know ways to prepare and create new flavors to enjoy.

Add some of your homemade herb breads or cakes to your gift basket. The small mini loaf pans are just the right size and a way of sharing some of your homemade goodies, too.

If you planned ahead and made herb vinegars from your garden, this is the time to decorate the bottles and include them with special notes for a hostess or when paying a holiday visit.

If you have a gardener on your shopping list who loves the flavor of fresh herbs, why not give them a collection of small herb plants to grow on a sunny windowsill. Fresh herb bouquets, wreaths, drying racks and garlic and herbs can all be gifts to enjoy fresh and use in the kitchen later.

My favorite plant for the holidays is rosemary. It stays green all winter long and just as the holidays approach, it starts to bloom for its new season's growth. Rosemary topiaries are fun to decorate with ornaments for a mini Christmas tree. And rosemary is for remembrance; that makes it an extra special gift from the heart.

Gardening is the number one family activity, and there are seed collections and books on gardening, especially for children. It's a great hands-on way for them to have fun while learning about the beauty and complexity of nature. It's a great gift for children and adults who work and play together.

Herbal Weddings

"All brides know that in matters of the heart and the hearth, Herbs make the difference."

—Bertha Reppert

The use of flowers and herbs in the celebration of a marriage goes back thousands of years. In ancient Greece, brides carried bouquets of fresh marjoram and wore crowns of fragrant myrtle. Brides in classical Rome wore rosemary and roses in their hair. In seventeenth century England, branches of rosemary were gilded, tied with flowing silk ribbons and carried before the bride as she proceeded to the church. In mid-Eastern countries, brides were adorned with gilded wheat and fragrant orange blossoms, symbols of wealth and fertility.

Traditions are the glue that helps bind societies together. The use of herbs and flowers in the marriage celebration, at the very formation of a new family, keeps ancient wedding tradition polished and usable, and glowing softly like a lovely piece of silver passed from generation to generation.

Herbs and flowers help to provide a joyful and thankful beginning to wedded life.

Wedding Herbs

There are five meaningful wedding herbs and plants—rosemary, myrtle, sweet marjoram, ivy and rue—that have historically been used in wedding ceremonies and are just as important today in modern herbal weddings.

Let's take an in-depth look at each of these wedding herbs with all their meanings and folklore.

Rosemary (rosemarinus officinalis): is perhaps the chief wedding herb. It has been used at marriages as a symbol of fidelity, loyalty and remembrance for at least 2,000 years. A quote from a wedding ceremony of 1607 says, "Let this rosemary, this flower of men, be a sign of your wisdom, love and loyalty, to be carried not only in your hands, but in your heads and hearts." A beautiful blessing and excellent advice.

Sprigs of fresh green rosemary can be used liberally throughout the wedding: in the wedding bouquet, the groom's boutonniere, the parents' flowers and the bridesmaids' bouquets. Large pots of rosemary can be used near the altar as well as at the reception. And if your wedding is in January, February or March, you get an extra bonus—this is when rosemary is in bloom and at its prettiest.

The bride should also be sure to take one of the pots of rosemary to her new home. A mixture of wedding herbs that consist of rosemary, marjoram, rose petals and other symbolic herbs can be put in beautiful baskets and passed around among the guests to use for showering the newlyweds as they leave for their honeymoon.

Sweet marjoram (origanum majorana): a symbol of joy and happiness, was a great favorite of the ancient Greeks and Romans. Wedding couples were crowned with wreaths of sweet marjoram. Brides carried bouquets of it and the path of the bride was commonly strewn with the fragrant green leaves. The Greeks so loved the scent of sweet marjoram that they burned it in the temples as a special incense to please the gods.

Myrtle (myrtus communis): is an aromatic shrub with tiny fragrant shiny dark leaves. Called true myrtle to distinguish it from Vinca or ground myrtle, it is an ancient emblem of Venus, a symbol of love and passion. Many cultures loved and used myrtle in weddings and on other festive occasions. The Bible refers to myrtle as a symbol of divine generosity. In England it stood for peace, home and restfulness and sprigs were added to bridal bouquets. German and Swedish brides wore crowns of myrtle. A medieval legend tells the story of Adam declaring his love to Eve in a grove of myrtle and then carrying a sprig with him as they were driven from Eden.

Rue (ruta graveolens): is the herb of vision, virtue and virginity. The latter may be slightly out of fashion today, but vision and virtue are still sorely needed blessings. In Latvia and Lithuania, rue is the most important of all herbs. On her wedding day, a bride wears a crown of rue leaves and after the ceremony, carries a pot of rue from her mother's garden to her new home.

Ivy (hedera helix): the symbol of friendship, fidelity and marriage, is still regularly used in wedding bouquets. Many brides love ivy and specifically request its use in their wedding flowers without ever knowing that common ivy was a most important green in weddings of 2,000 years ago.

Because ivy was sacred to both Hymen, god of marriage and the wedding feast, and Dionysus, god of wine and festivity, bridal altars in ancient Greece were wreathed with strands of ivy. In classical Rome, newly-married couples were presented with a lush bough of ivy which they both held to symbolize their union and friendship. A nice idea and one, perhaps, we should revive.

Any and all ivy can be used at a wedding. There are a variety of leaf sizes as well as colors from a solid, rich dark green to many variations of white and green. It can be used by the leaf, sprig, strand or plant. It holds up well in and out of water.

Other herbs and flowers are lovely and meaningful additions to an herbal wedding. Using the following herbs and flowers, you can create a bridal bouquet or arrangement with a combination of sentimental meanings:

For joy:

Marjoram—joy and happiness
Heart's ease—happy thoughts
Burnet—a merry heart
Mugwort—happiness
Parsley—festivity

For love:

Roses—love and desire
Blue salvia—I think of you
Mints—warmth of feeling
Myrtle—love and passion
Lavender—devotion

For the future:

Sage—long life, good health and domestic virtue
Southernwood—constancy and perseverance
Rue—vision and virtue
Rosemary—remembrance and fidelity
Chamomile—patience
Thyme—strength and courage
Ivy—friendship and fidelity

❧

Be sure to have these seven blessing herbs worked into the wedding flowers:

Rosemary—Bless this wedding!
Bay—Bless the groom!
Myrtle—Bless the bride!
Fennel—Bless the baby!

Catnip—Bless the kitty!
Basil—Bless this home!
Angelica—Bless us all!

There are certainly a great many combinations possible depending on the philosophy of the bridal couple, the time of the year and what fresh flowers and herbs may be available.

Cutting Herbs and Flowers For The Wedding

If you plan to use plant material from your garden, it can be cut 48 hours before the wedding. Arm your floral gathering committee with sharp clippers and shears, plenty of buckets partially filled with warm water, and a hammer for crushing stems so they will take up more water, keeping the flowers perky.

The ideal time to pick is in the early morning when the herbs and flowers are in peak condition. As the day warms up, the plants tend to droop. Cut twice as much material as you estimate you will need. It's wiser to have too much than too little.

Using Herbs In The Wedding

The sentiment, symbolism and tradition should be carried throughout the wedding party in bouquet, boutonnieres, corsages, flowers for the church, the reception and the wedding meal.

The most important person at the wedding is, of course, the bride. Her bouquet is the floral centerpiece that sets the tone for the entire wedding. All the other flowers should complement and accent it. Because of the symbolism involved in an herbal wedding, it is important for the bride to consider carefully what she wants her bouquet to say. Ideally, it should sing with joy and blush with love, yet cast a thoughtful eye on the realities of marriage.

Fresh or dried flower petals and herbs can be carried in a basket for the flower girl to drop as the bride walks down the aisle of the church. Herbs and flower petals can be tossed in place of rice for fragrance and sentiment; a combination of roses for love, rosemary for remembrance, marjoram for happiness and lavender for devotion would be colorful and fragrant as the bridal couple leaves the church. In fact, bags of wedding herbs and flowers can be given to the guests at the church for just that purpose.

Herbs can be used to fill ring pillows (it's best to use them dried or use a potpourri). You can set the scene with herbal wreaths on the doors of the church or home. Fresh herbs can be used as candle rings at the church as well as centerpieces at the reception. Herbs and colorful flowers can also make ideal napkin rings. And certainly a rosemary halo for the bride's hair is truly a crowning glory.

Centerpieces of fresh herbs and flowers can be used for the bridal shower and after the party, the guests of honor can use them as colorful and fragrant decorations in their home. Be sure to label the herbs so that people know what they are and why the bridal couple chose to use them. They should express the traditional bridal wishes for health, love and prosperity.

Sheaves of wheat, a symbol of plenty and fruitfulness, combined with herbs can be effective for a fall wedding as centerpieces and decorations for the church and reception.

In addition to the many flowers that are growing in your garden, pots of flowers and herbs can be used for decorating along pathways. By using potted plants, you have the freedom to move them around where you want them, from the church to the reception. They also make lovely gifts for special friends and family members to take home as a remembrance. Topiaries of herbs are also something special that can be used.

For a summer poolside reception, a styrofoam square can be covered with herbs and flowers to float in a pool to add beauty to the scene.

Other herbal ideas:

-Enclose a fresh herb sprig with invitations and announcements.

-If you can write your own ceremony, mention your wedding herbs and flowers wherever appropriate.

-Print the list of your chosen herbs and their symbolism in the wedding program.

-Ask your photographer to include herbal vignettes among the wedding pictures to enhance your album of memories of this special day.

-If June is your month, use rose petals from your garden which can be mixed in with the rice.

-A large rectangular herbal sachet can be made for the kneeling bench for the church ceremony—as you kneel on the fragrance pillow it will release glorious aromas into the air.

-Use fresh mint leaves in the baskets carried by the flower girls.

-Be sure to place a bouquet of fragrant herbs and flowers by the guest book and tie a sprig of rosemary on the pen.

-Tie a bunch of herbs to the cake knife.

Be creative—the list can go on and on as to how to use herbs for your wedding.

And when the festivities are over, create a wonderful long-lasting remembrance by drying the herbs and flowers from your bridal bouquet and mixing them into a wedding bouquet potpourri. The traditional herbs of love, fidelity and happiness can be mixed with the predominately white colored flowers from a traditional wedding bouquet to display and scent your new life together.

Wedding Bouquet Potpourri

1 quart mixed white and pink dried rose petals, orange blossoms, myrtle flowers, white hydrangea flowers and pink rosebuds as well as any other flowers from the bridal bouquet
2 ounces mixed myrtle leaves, basil leaves, rose leaves and marjoram leaves
1 ounce rosemary
1 ounce finely ground gumbenzoin
1 ounce orris root powder
1 crushed cardamom seed
1 teaspoon crushed cassia
3 drops rose oil
3 drops lavender oil
1 drop patchouli oil

Put flowers, herb leaves, rosemary, gumbenzoin, orris root, cardamom seed and cassia in a large enameled bowl. Mix well with hands or a wooden spoon.

Add drops of oil, stirring continuously. Put mixture into sealed containers or jars. Leave in a cool, dark place to cure for several weeks before using.

Guests rarely forget an herbal wedding!

———————————————— ❧ ————————————————

Fresh herbs will add that very quiet dignity of their symbolism along with a lovely and thoughtful touch to your special day. While carrying your bouquet of fragrant herbs, think of their ancient symbolism, for herbs whisper a romantic sonnet that will sustain you for a lifetime of wedded bliss.

Resource Guide

I have put together a list based upon my experiences of where to find things. It is by no means all inclusive and represents some sources whom I have found to have great products from seeds to plants to supplies.

Abundant Life Seed Foundation, PO Box 772, Port Townsend, WA 98368
    mail order open pollinated seed catalog

Bluestone Perennials, 7211 Middle Ridge, Madison, OH 44057
    mail order catalog—plants

Bountiful Gardens, 18001 Shafer Ranch Rd., Willits, CA 95490
    mail order catalog, seeds, books, supplies

Caprilands Herb Farm, 534 Silver Street, Coventry, CT 06405
    mail order catalog, books, gardens, luncheons, gift shop

Clark's Greenhouse and Herbal Country, RR1 Box 15B, San Jose, IL 62682
    mail order catalog, plants, gardens, classes, gift shop

Companion Plants, 7247 N Coalville Ridge Rd., Athens, OH 45701
    mail order catalog, exotic herb seeds and plants

The Cook's Garden, PO Box 535, Londonderry, VT 05148
    mail order catalog, seeds, books, supplies

Davidson-Wilson Greenhouses, Inc., Rt 2 Box 168, Dept.46, Crawfordsville, IN 47933
    mail order catalog, specialty scented geraniums

Enchanted Crest, RR1 Box 216, Belle Rive, IL 62810
    display gardens, Bed and Breakfast, tours

Fox Hill Farm, 440 W. Michigan Ave., Parma, MI 49269
    mail order catalog, classes, gardens, gifts

The Gathered Herb and Greenhouse, 12114 N. State Rd. Dept HGP, Otisville, MI 48463
    mail order catalog, plants, gifts shop

Gilberties Herb Gardens, PO Box 118, Easton, CT 06612
    plants, classes

Heirloom Herbs, 1828 Fairmont Dr., Springfield, IL 62702
    retail plants, gift shop

The Herb Farm, 32804 ISSAQUAH-Fall City Rd., Fall City, WA 98024
    mail order catalog, plants, gift shop, classes, luncheons, gardens

J.W.Jung Seed and Nursery, 335 S. High St., Randolph, WI 53957
    mail order catalog, seeds and plants

Lily of the Valley Herb Farm, 3969 Fox Ave., Minerva, OH 44657.
    mail order catalog, plants, gifts

Logee's Greenhouse, 141 North Street, Danielson, CT 06239
 mail order catalog, exotic herbs

The Natural Garden, 38W443 Highway 64, St. Charles, IL 60175
 retail herbs

Nichols Garden Nursery, 1190 North Pacific Hwy., Albany, OR 97321
 mail order seeds, gifts

Pinetree Garden Seeds, Box 300, New Gloucester, ME 04260
 mail order catalog, seeds, books, supplies

Richters, Goodwood, ON, Loc, 1AD, Canada
 mail order catalog, seeds and plants, books, etc. extensive offerings

The Rosemary House, 120 S Market Street, Mechanicsburg, PA 17055
 mail order catalog, seeds, plants, gifts, etc.

Sandy Mush Herb Nursery, RT 2 Surrett Cove Rd., Leicester, NC 28748
 mail order catalog, plants, seeds, books

Seeds of Change, 621 Old Santa Fe Trail #10, Santa Fe, NM 87501
 mail order catalog, certified organic seeds, gardens

Shady Acres Herb Farm, 7815 Hwy 212, Chaska, MN 55318
 mail order catalog, plants, seeds, gifts, classes

Shepherd's Garden Seeds, 6116 Highway 9 #1, Felton, CA 95018
 mail order catalog, plants, seeds, supplies

Stella Natura Agricultural Calendar BioDynamic Farming & Gardening Assn.,
 PO Box 550, Kimberton, PA 19442

Thyme from Rosemary, N6535 State Road 120, Elkhorn, WI 53121
 mail order catalog, plants, gifts, wreaths, etc., gardens, luncheons

Magazines and Reference Guides

Green Prints, Box 1355 Fairview, NC 28730

The Herb Companion, Interweave Press, 201 East Fourth St., Loveland, CO 80537

The Herb Companion Wish Book and Resource Guide (same address as above)

The Herbal Connection, Herb Growing and Marketing Network,
PO Box 245, Silver Springs, PA 17575

The Herb Quarterly, PO box 689, San Anselmo, CA 94960

Northwind Farm's Herb Resource Directory, Northwind Farm Publications,
RT 2 Box 246, Shevlin, MN 56676

Bibliography

Barash, Cathy Wilkinson. *Edible Flowers From Garden to Palate.* Golden, CO:
Fulcrum Publishing, 1993.

Boxer, Arabella and Phillippa Back. *The Herb Book.* New York: Gallery Books, 1989.

Bremness, Lesley. *RD Home Handbooks Herbs.* Pleasantville, NY:
The Reader's Digest Association, Inc., 1990.

Campbell, Stu. *Let It Rot.* Pownal, VT: Storey Communications, Inc., 1989.

Dille, Carolyn and Susan Bellsinger. *Herbs in the Kitchen.* Loveland, CO:
Interweave Press, Inc., 1992.

Exley, Helen, ed. *Garden Lovers Quotations.* Waterford, United Kingdom:
Exley Publications Ltd, 1992.

Gardens—Quotations On The Perennial Pleasures Of Soil, Seed and Sun. Compiled by Holly Hughes.
Philadelphia: Running Press, 1994.

Garland, Sarah. *The Complete Book of Herbs & Spices.* Pleasantville, NY:
The Reader's Digest Association, Inc., 1993.

Gilbertie, Sal. *Herb Gardening At Its Best.* New York: Antheneum, 1978.

Holt, Geraldene. *Geraldene Holt's Complete Book of Herbs.* New York:
Henry Holt & Company, 1991.

Jones, Julia and Barbara Deer. *The Country Diary of Garden Lore.* New York:
Summit Books, 1990.

Lima, Patricia. *The Harrowsmith Illustrated Book of Herbs.* Ontario, Canada:
Camden House, 1990.

McLeod, Judyth A. *Lavender, Sweet Lavender.* Kenthurst: Kangaroo Press, 1989.

Riotte, Louise. *Carrots Love Tomatoes.* Pownal, VT: Storey Communications, Inc., 1992.
—. *Roses Love Garlic.* Pownal, VT: Storey Communications, Inc., 1990.
—. *Sleeping With A Sunflower.* Pownal, VT: Storey Communications, Inc., 1987.

Rodale's Illustrated Encyclopedia of Herbs. Emmaus, PA: Rodale Press, 1987.

Simmons, Adelma Grenier. *The Book of Valentine Remembrances.* Coventry, CT:
Caprilands Herb Farm.
—. *A Garden Walk.* Coventry, CT: Caprilands Herb Farm.
—. *Saints In The Garden.* Coventry, CT: Caprilands Herb Farm.
—. *A Witches Brew.* Coventry, CT: Caprilands Herb Farm.

Staff of Organic Gardening Magazine. *The Encyclopedia of Organic Gardening.* Emmaus, PA:
Rodale Press, 1978.

Tolley, Emelie and Chris Mead. *Herbs, Gardens, Decorations and Recipes.* New York:
Clarkson L. Potter Inc., Publishers, 1985.

Wyman, Donald. *Wyman's Gardening Encyclopedia,* Second Edition. New York:
McMillan Publishing, 1986.

Index

Bold page numbers denote a feature in Herbs in Profile and will include herb illustration, description, best growing conditions, etc.

Recipe Index

❧

To order

***Growing and Using Herbs
in the Midwest***

or for a free catalog of
other Amherst Press
Books-To-Go titles,
call toll free
1-800-333-8122